"*Augsburg is to be commended for providing an intelligent opening for an informed and sensitive dialogue between Jews and Christians.*"

Rabbi Leon Klenicki
Director, Department of Interfaith Affairs
Anti-Defamation League of B'nai B'rith

JUDAISM:
An Introduction for Christians

JAMES LIMBURG
translator & editor

AUGSBURG Publishing House • Minneapolis

Library of Congress Cataloging-in-Publication Data

Was jeder vom Judentum wissen muss. English.
  JUDAISM: AN INTRODUCTION FOR CHRISTIANS.

  Translation of: Was jeder vom Judentum wissen muss.
  Bibliography: p.
  Includes index.
  1. Judaism.   2. Jews—North America.   3. Christianity
and other religions—Judaism.   4. Judaism—Relations—
Christianity.   I. Limburg, James, 1935–
II. Title.
BM561.W3613   1987   296'.0242   87-9189
ISBN 0-8066-2263-6

Manufactured in the U.S.A.   APH 10-3610

   2   3   4   5   6   7   8   9   0   1   2   3   4   5   6   7   8   9

Contents

Preface

The title of this book accurately describes its contents and the purpose for which it was written: *Judaism: An Introduction for Christians.* This is a book about Judaism. As an *introduction,* it has a quite specific purpose. A host introducing two guests will identify some things that the guests have in common, hoping in this way to aid the guests in striking up a conversation. This book intends to function in the manner of a host, introducing Christian readers to Judaism. In so doing, it often points out things that Christians and Jews have in common, hoping thereby to get a conversation going.

This book is an introduction *for Christians.* Anyone is welcome to read it, of course. But all should be aware that it is aimed at Christian readers who know very little about Judaism, "the root that supports you," as Paul put it (Rom. 11:18). Jewish readers may feel that important things have been left out or that Jewish teachings and practices are at times described too much in Christian terms; but the book was designed to communicate to Christian readers, and therefore it uses language and concepts that they will understand.

After an introduction that tells the story of the settlement of Jews in North America and then recalls the broad outlines of their history, the book divides into three major parts. The first of these focuses on Israel (Chapters 3-7), the second on Jewish faith and life (Chapters 8-16), and the last on Christians and Jews, with special attention to the person of Jesus (Chapters 17-25). A final section includes five important statements on Christian-Jewish relationships. Suggested study questions and recommendations for further investigation are found at the end of the book.

This book originated in West Germany as a series of pamphlets which were designed to provide new insights into Judaism for ordinary people. Under the leadership of Pastor Arnulf H. Baumann, working groups of the United Evangelical Lutheran Church of Germany and the German National Committee of the Lutheran World Federation began to produce individual pieces on specific themes, which were then distributed as supplements to a quarterly publication devoted to Jewish-Christian concerns. The first pamphlet appeared in 1976, and the response was astonishing. More and more copies were requested as the simply-written pieces were used in congregational study groups, confirmation classes, religion classes in the schools, and a variety of other settings. Jewish congregations distributed them to Christian visitors to their synagogues.

The number of pamphlets in the series grew to 25. Beginning with the second pamphlet, each was read not only by members of the working group but also by rabbis and other Jewish persons. The series has continued to grow in popularity in Germany, with total publication now in the millions.

Finally, the pamphlets were gathered and edited by Pastor Baumann into a book entitled, *Was jeder vom Judentum wissen muss* (What Everyone Ought to Know about Judaism). The book was first published in 1983.

This North American edition is a translation and adaptation of the third German edition published in 1985. A number of additions and alterations have been made to suit the new audience. For example, a chapter on the history of Judaism in North America has been substituted for similar chapters on Judaism in Germany. In addition to the work of the American editor, the consultation team, and editors from Augsburg Publishing House, the manuscript has been reviewed by a number of additional readers, both Jews and Christians. These reviewers made many helpful suggestions.

Our hope is that this edition of the book will be as useful to the English-speaking world as the original has been in Germany.

I wish to thank the various individuals, both Jewish and Christian, who have read through the manuscript, made comments on it, and responded to my questions. A special word of thanks goes to our son David, a graduate student in German at the Ohio State University, who spent a good part of a summer checking the translation.

James Limburg

PART ONE

INTRODUCING THE JEWS

1

The Jews in North America

On the base of the Statue of Liberty is a poem written by Emma Lazarus, a Jewish woman from New York. The poem welcomes immigrants to America with these words:

Give me your tired, your poor,
Your huddled masses, yearning to breathe free,
The wretched refuse of your teeming shore.
Send these, the homeless, tempest-tost to me,
I lift my lamp beside the golden door!

Among the tired and the poor, the homeless and the tempest-tossed who emigrated to America have been millions of Jews.

The total number of Jews in the United States today is estimated at 5.8 million, or about 2.5% of the total population. The percentage is small, but the impact of these people on life in the U.S. and in the world community has been great. To name a few more or less contemporary examples: former Secretary of State Henry Kissinger and former Supreme Court Justice Arthur Goldberg; writers Saul Bellow and Isaac Bashhevis Singer, Chaim Potok and Herman Wouk; scientists Albert Einstein and Jonas Salk; astronaut Judith Resnik; theological thinkers Abraham Joshua Heschel and Elie Wiesel; violinists Jascha Heifetz and Isaac Stern; pianists Vladimir Horowitz and Artur Rubinstein; composers and performers Aaron Copland and

Leonard Bernstein, Irving Berlin and Richard Rodgers, George Gershwin and Victor Borge, Bob Dylan and Beverly Sills.

There are some 310,000 Jews in Canada, making up 1.2% of the population. There, too, the impact of Jewish persons has been significant. Examples include former Chief Justice of the Supreme Court of Canada Bora Laskin and former Premier of British Columbia David Barrett; poet and songwriter Leonard Cohen and novelist Mordecai Richler; theological thinker and scholar Emil Fackenheim; television personalities Lorne Greene and Rich Little; sculptor Sorel Etrog and painter Gerald Gladstone; conductor Boris Brott.

How did it happen that Jews settled in North America? Where did they come from? What are their attitudes toward the religious traditions and practices of their forebears? Such questions will concern us in this chapter.

Sephardic Jews in the Colonial Period (1654–1776)

The first Jews to settle in North America were refugees from Recife, Brazil, who landed in New Amsterdam (later New York) in 1654. They were Sephardic Jews, that is, Jews of Spanish-Portuguese origin, part of a group that had left Europe in order to escape persecution and to find new opportunities. When the Portuguese took Brazil from the Dutch in 1654, the Jews living there were given three months to leave. Most went to Holland, but one ship carrying 23 Jews eventually found its way to New Amsterdam.

Conditions for this minority group living in New Amsterdam under Peter Stuyvesant were barely tolerable. When the English took over in 1664 and New

Amsterdam became New York, things improved somewhat. The first synagogue, Shearith Israel (The Remnant of Israel), was built in 1730. Though the original building no longer survives, the congregation is still in existence.

The earliest Jewish settlers coming to America were mainly of Sephardic background. In 1763 a group of them built a synagogue in Newport, Rhode Island, which still stands as the oldest surviving Jewish house of worship in the United States. Other early Jewish communities were founded in Charleston, South Carolina; Savannah, Georgia; and Philadelphia, Pennsylvania.

The earliest congregation in Canada was also Sephardic. Jews from the 13 colonies, mainly merchants and those associated with fur trading, settled in Montreal. There they established a synagogue, known as the Spanish and Portuguese Synagogue, in 1768. It took the name of the first synagogue established in New York City: Shearith Israel. Montreal soon became the center for Jewish life in Canada and remains, along with Toronto and, to a lesser degree, Winnipeg, one of the three largest Jewish communities in that country.

The situation for Jews in other U.S. colonies was different from what it was in those already mentioned. Maryland was formed as a haven for Catholics, with a law that excluded those who did not believe in Jesus Christ. In Virginia, the Church of England was strong, and no early Jewish community developed.

Puritan Massachusetts had no Jewish community, but there was a strong Hebrew influence because of the impact of the Bible, especially the Old Testament. The Puritans saw themselves as the new Israelites and America as the new promised land. Their only king was God. The Old Testament became the basis for their laws and played an important part in everyday living:

Their names were often Biblical and like Jews they observed the Sabbath and other holidays from sundown to sundown. Like Orthodox Jews today they refrained from all work on the Sabbath. Their feasts often developed from Jewish holidays. Thanksgiving was patterned after the Jewish harvest celebration of *Sukkot*. While Puritan practice did not always derive from Jewish precedent, Puritans were fully aware of the many similarities between their religion and Judaism.

(*Jews in American History* by Jerome Ruderman, KTAV, 1974, p. 34)

The importance of the Hebrew Bible was also evident in education. Hebrew was taught at Harvard as early as 1655 and was required at Yale. Massachusetts Governor William Bradford's beginning Hebrew book is still in existence, with his name and the date, 1652, on the front cover. When the Liberty Bell was installed in Philadelphia, in 1753, on it was an inscription taken from the Hebrew Scriptures: "Proclaim liberty throughout all the land unto the inhabitants thereof" (Lev. 25:10). One historian expresses the impact of the Hebrew Bible on early American history this way:

For an American Jew, it is exhilarating to contemplate that the great principles upon which this nation was founded were based on a book the Christian world knows as the Old Testament, the product of Jewish genius. Thus, the greatest contribution to the spirit and founding of America was made not by American Jews, but by a book by their forefathers, written over two millennia before the existence of the American continent was known.

(*The Jews in America* by Max Dimont, Simon and Schuster, 1978, p. 54)

A few summary observations about Jews in the colonial period: The number of Jewish immigrants during this time was small. One estimate is that on the eve of the American Revolution, there were about 2000 Jews out of a population of three million Americans, or less than a tenth of one percent. The first of these Jewish immigrants had origins in Spain and Portugal. They had not come out of the European ghettos, and this made them different from the German Jews soon to follow. These Sephardic-American Jews dressed like their neighbors, participated in community life to the degree that was possible, and soon became a part of the middle class. Congregations were formed and led by lay people, with no rabbis arriving until the mid-1800s. The Hebrew Bible (the Christian Old Testament) had a major impact on life in the colonies, especially in Puritan Massachusetts.

German Jews and Reform Judaism (1820–1880)

When the Revolutionary War broke out in 1775, most American Jews, who had little connection with England, were on the side of the revolutionaries. Though the Canadian Jews had ties with relatives in the Colonies, most of them sided with the British. Many Jews in the Colonies fought in the Continental army. One of the provisions of the constitution, ratified not long after the war, was a prohibition against the federal government establishing any religion. This helped to secure freedom of religion for all citizens. In 1790, the Jewish congregation of Newport, Rhode Island, wrote to President Washington commending him on the achievement of this new religious freedom. A portion of Washington's reply reads as follows:

The Citizens of the United States of America have a right to applaud themselves for having given to mankind examples of an enlarged and liberal policy, a policy worthy of imitation.

All possess alike liberty of conscience and immunities of citizenship. It is now no more that toleration is spoken of, as if it was by the indulgence of one class of people, that another enjoyed the exercise of their inherent natural rights. For happily the government of the United States, which gives to bigotry no sanction, to persecution no assistance, requires only that they who live under its protection should demean themselves as good citizens, in giving it on all occasions their effectual support. . . .

May the children of the Stock of Abraham, who dwell in this land, continue to merit and enjoy the good will of the other inhabitants, while every one shall sit in safety under his own vine and fig-tree, and there shall be none to make him afraid. . . .

(*Readings in Modern Jewish History* by Eliezer L. Ehrmann, KTAV, 1977, p. 344)

Jews living in the new nation did enjoy freedom from persecution and experienced remarkable growth in numbers. European Jews at this time, especially in German lands, were leaving because of persecution at home and the promise of new opportunities in America. The *Encyclopaedia Judaica* estimates that in 1820 there were 4000 Jews in the United States. By 1880, that number had grown to 280,000. The Jewish people began to move across the continent, with communities established in cities such as Cleveland and Chicago, Detroit and Milwaukee, Louisville and Minneapolis, St. Louis and New Orleans. Jews participated in the Gold Rush; in 1849 they held a Yom Kippur service in San Francisco, and by 1850 two congregations had been formed in that city.

Jewish settlement in Canada was very slow. The first Ashkenazic (one of the two main types of European Judaism) congregation, made up of immigrants from England, Poland, and Germany, had its beginnings in Montreal in 1846. It took the name Shaar Hashomayim or "Gate of Heaven." Canadian Jews also moved westward in search of gold. A Jewish community was founded in Victoria, British Columbia, in 1859. The number of Jews in Canada remained small. It is estimated that 100 years after the founding of the Montreal synagogue in 1768, there were still only about 700 Jews in all of Canada (*Encyclopaedia Judaica*).

Like other mid-19th century immigrants, many Jews became peddlers. They began by traveling across the countryside with their wares on their backs. The next move was to a horse and buggy, and then, eventually, some would settle down to found retail operations. Stores such as Macy's, Bloomingdale's, and Gimbel's, as well as countless small stores scattered across the nation, had their beginnings in this way. Levi Strauss, for example, was one of these Jewish peddlers, and he began by selling his denim "Levis" to miners in California.

These years saw the flourishing of Reform Judaism in America. This movement had its beginnings in Germany, greatly influenced by the ideas of Moses Mendelssohn (1717–1786), the grandfather of the composer, Felix. Moses Mendelssohn has been referred to by historians as "the Jewish Luther." He was afraid that the Judaism of the ghettos in his day was about to stagnate and die. Jews had to get out of the ghettos and into the mainstream of European life. But if they did so too quickly, Mendelssohn believed, they would leave their Judaism behind. So Mendelssohn translated the Torah (the first five books of the Bible) from Hebrew into German. He encouraged Jews to use German instead of Yiddish, the language of the ghetto. He advocated a number of accommodations to the modern age.

This kind of updated Judaism fit the American scene very well. Most of the German Jewish immigrants had come out of isolated ghettos. Suddenly they found themselves in an entirely new situation. What would this mean for their religion? Since Orthodox Judaism in the new land allowed for little or no accommodation to the new environment, it became an option for only a very few. Leaders of the Jewish communities in America believed that adjustments had to be made or Judaism would die out in the new land. The leader of the American Reform movement was Rabbi Isaac Mayer Wise, an immigrant from Bohemia who eventually became a rabbi in Cincinnati in 1854. Soon he was at the center of the Reform movement. Max Dimont lists some of Wise's innovations: He introduced the mixed choir, the organ, and the family pew. He eliminated the mandatory wearing of hats during the service. He preached in English and aimed his sermons at the concrete needs of his people. He published an American Prayerbook in which the service was almost exclusively in English. This shift from Hebrew to English had profound implications for Jewish education and Jewish identity. Rabbi Wise helped to organize the

Union of American Hebrew Congregations and founded Hebrew Union College in Cincinnati in 1875. Dimont summarizes the results of the efforts of Wise and
other Reform leaders:

By 1880, American Reform Judaism reigned supreme in
the land. It had subdued the Orthodox, organized its own
rambunctious congregations, established the first successful
rabbinic college, and ringed the continent with a string of
magnificent Reform temples . . . [Wise] united America's
Jews and enabled them to assert that they were Jews, that
they were modern, and that they were American.

(*The Jews in America,* pp. 138, 143)

The beliefs of American Reform Judaism were summarized in the "Pittsburgh Platform" of 1885, prepared at a conference chaired by Wise. The following
excerpts suggest something of the spirit of Reform
Judaism at this time:

Moral Laws

We recognize in the Mosaic legislation a system of training the Jewish people for its mission during its national life
in Palestine, and to-day we accept as binding only the moral
laws, and maintain only such ceremonies as elevate and
sanctify our lives, but reject all such as are not adapted to
the views and habits of modern civilization.

Laws No Longer Valid

We hold that all such Mosaic and rabbinical laws as regulate diet, priestly purity, and dress, originated in ages and
under the influence of ideas altogether foreign to our present
mental and spiritual state. They fail to impress the modern
Jew with a spirit of priestly holiness; their observance in

our days is apt rather to obstruct than to further modern spiritual elevation.

No Longer a Nation

We recognize, in the modern era of universal culture of heart and intellect, the approaching of the realization of Israel's great Messianic hope for the establishment of the kingdom of trust, justice and peace among all men. We consider ourselves no longer a nation, but a religious community and therefore expect neither a return to Palestine, nor a sacrificial worship under the sons of Aaron, nor the restoration of any of the laws concerning the Jewish state.

A Progressive Religion

We recognize in Judaism a progressive religion, ever striving to be in accord with the postulates of reason. We are convinced of the utmost necessity of preserving the historical identity with our great past. . . .

(*Readings in Modern Jewish History,* p. 38)

Fifty years later, Reform rabbis met in Columbus, Ohio, and formulated the "Columbus Platform," which reflected a difference in emphasis, particularly in a section affirming the development of "A Jewish Homeland."

In summary, during the century that followed American independence, the number of Jews in the United States grew from a few thousand to more than a quarter of a million. Jewish immigrants were a part of the great migration to the west and established themselves in communities, mostly cities, across the land. While Jews experienced some discrimination in the new land, they were free from the savage persecutions they had known in Europe and enjoyed freedom of religion. An

American brand of Reform Judaism seemed ideally suited to the American situation and had won the day. Jewish population in Canada was very small, with some 2,393 reported in the 1881 census (*Encyclopaedia Judaica*).

Eastern European Jews and the Conservative Movement (1880–1940)

The years after 1880 saw a great wave of Jewish immigration from eastern European countries, including Russia, Poland, Hungary, and Rumania. The reasons for emigration were the familiar ones: Jews experienced intensive persecution in the Russian pogroms of the early 1880s. Also, there was the problem of finding space for the growing number of Jews to make a living. Crushing poverty and lack of freedom plagued Jews, as well as other Europeans. North America beckoned as a land of opportunity, and improved rail and steamship transportation brought the dream of going there within reach.

The Jewish population in the United States grew from just over a quarter of a million in 1880 to some four and one-half million by 1925, the year when the U.S. government imposed limits on immigration. After about the year 1940, the majority of Jews in the nation would be native born. The population of Jews in Canada also reflected the impact of the pogroms in Eastern Europe. In the years after 1882, a good number of congregations were founded in eastern Canada, and also in the west; in Toronto in 1883; Hamilton in 1887; Winnipeg in 1882 and 1885; Calgary in 1905; Brandon in 1900; Edmonton in 1911 (*Encyclopaedia Judaica*).

What were the feelings of these immigrants as they left their homelands and set out for a new life in America? In his novel, *The Rise of David Levinsky,* Abraham Cahan describes the arrival of a young immigrant:

I was one of a multitude of steerage passengers on a Bremen steamship on my way to New York. Who can depict the feeling of desolation, homesickness, uncertainty, and anxiety with which an emigrant makes his first voyage across the ocean? I proved to be a good sailor, but the sea frightened me. The thumping of the engines was drumming a ghastly accompaniment to the awesome whisper of the waves. I felt in the embrace of a vast, uncanny force . . . .

In my devotions, which I performed three times a day, without counting a benediction before every meal and every drink of water, grace after every meal and a prayer before going to sleep, I would mentally plead for the safety of the ship and for a speedy sight of land. My scanty luggage included a pair of phylacteries and a plump little prayer book with the *Book of Psalms* at the end. The prayers I knew by heart, but I now often said psalms, in addition, particularly when the sea looked angry and the pitching or rolling was unusually violent. I read all kinds of psalms, but my favorite among them was the 104th, generally referred to by our people as "Bless the Lord, O my soul," its opening words in the original Hebrew. It is a poem on the power and wisdom of God as manifested in the wonders of nature, some of its verses dealing with the sea. It is said by the faithful every Saturday afternoon including the fall and winter; so I have recited it from memory, but I preferred to read it in my prayer book. For it seemed as though the familiar words had changed their identity and meaning, especially those concerned with the sea. Their divine inspiration was now something visible and audible. It was not I who was reading them. It was as though the waves and the clouds, the whole far-flung scene of restlessness and mystery, were whispering to me:

"Thou who coverest thyself with light as with a garment, who stretchest out the heavens like a curtain; who layest the beams of his chambers in the waters: who maketh the clouds his chariot: who walketh upon the wings of the wind . . . . So is this great and wide sea wherein are things creeping and innumerable, both small and great beasts. There go the ships: there is that leviathan whom thou hast made to play therein . . . ."

When the discoverers of America saw land at last they fell on their knees and a hymn of thanksgiving burst from their souls. The scene, which is one of the most thrilling in history, repeats itself in the heart of every immigrant as he comes in sight of the American shores. I am at a loss to convey the particular state of mind that the experience created in me . . . .

"This, then, is America!" I exclaimed, mutely. The notion of something enchanted which the name had always evoked in me now seemed fully borne out.

In my ecstasy I could not help thinking of Psalm 104, and, opening my little prayer book, I glanced over those of its verses that speak of hills and rocks, of grass and trees and birds. When I reached the words, "I will sing to the Lord as long as I live: I will sing praises to my God while I have my being," I uttered them in a fervent whisper. . . .

How did the David Levinskys and their families who reached America make a living? With the establishment of retail stores across the land, the day of the peddler was past. A great number found work in the garment industries, in New York and in other cities. Some became leaders in labor movements growing out of these industries. Others became a part of the work force in a whole variety of occupations across the continent. In California, Jewish immigrant families with names such as Mayer, Selznick, and Warner became pioneers in the film industry.

The language of these eastern European immigrants was Yiddish, basically German with a good number of Hebrew and eastern European words thrown in, and written with Hebrew letters. During the 1920s, Yiddish culture flourished, with Yiddish theaters, schools, and newspapers. As a new generation arose which spoke more and more English, Yiddish died out, but not without enriching American English with such words as *chutzpah* (gall, nerve), *zaftig* (pleasingly plump), *klutz* (a clumsy person), and the like (see *The Joys of Yiddish* by Leo Rosten for a delightful introduction to Yiddish language, culture, and humor).

During this time there were outbreaks of anti-Semitism (hatred of Jews), mostly in the form of discrimination against Jews in the workplace. Certain large companies and banks would not hire Jews. Colleges and universities had quotas for the number of Jewish students to be admitted; admission to medical schools was especially difficult. Jewish doctors were not allowed on hospital staffs. Clubs and neighborhoods declared themselves off-limits for Jews. In the 1920s, automaker Henry Ford published an anti-Jewish tract entitled *The International Jew.* Millions of copies were circulated, and it had considerable influence; Ford finally apologized and retracted what he had written. The Ku Klux Klan also became involved in some anti-Jewish actions.

A great number of Jewish organizations were founded during this period. World War I gave additional impetus to American Zionism, and several Zionist organizations were formed. The Young Men's and Young Women's Hebrew Associations, patterned after the YMCA and YWCA, had their beginnings in 1854. Other organizations which began at this time were the Hadassah Society (1912), the Hillel Foundation (1923), the Anti-Defamation League of B'nai B'rith (1913) and, after the depression in 1929, the United Jewish Appeal (1939). In Canada, the first B'nai B'rith lodge was chartered in Toronto in 1875. The Zionist Organization of Canada was in existence in 1900. Hadassah organized in 1916. In 1919 the Canadian Jewish Congress was assembled, an organization which has come to represent all sectors of the Jewish community. These and countless similar organizations gave Jews who did not wish to affiliate with a synagogue (as well as Jews who did belong to a synagogue) a chance to express their Jewishness in their new environment.

What about the religious beliefs and practices of these eastern European immigrants? The majority of them came from Orthodox backgrounds and were traditional in their Judaism when they arrived (as illustrated by the excerpt from Cahan's book). But many of these immigrants did not feel at home with the extremely conservative Orthodox congregations in America. Nor were they comfortable with the somewhat radical American Reform movement. The one group seemed incompatible with modern life, the other irresponsible toward its Jewish heritage. Thus in 1887, the Jewish Theological Seminary was formed in New York City as the place to train rabbis in a new "Conservative" Judaism which would steer a middle course between Reform and Orthodoxy. Especially under the leadership of Solomon Schechter in the early 1900s, the Conservative seminary flourished and the Conservative movement grew.

In summary, the mass immigration of eastern European Jews after 1880 changed the shape and style of North American Judaism. As these more traditional Jews mixed in with the prevailing German-Jewish culture in America, Reform Judaism no longer dominated. Orthodoxy was given new support with the influx of a large number of Orthodox rabbis from Eastern Europe. The Conservative movement was born. Numerous philanthropic and Zionist organizations were founded; for some Jews, these groups became their exclusive involvement in Jewish life. The United States, with the largest concentration of Jews of any country on earth, had become an important center for world Jewry. Canada's Jewish population had increased dramatically, from 2,393 in 1881 to some 168,000 in 1941. Montreal, Toronto, and, to a lesser degree, Winnipeg, emerged as the centers for Jewish population.

American Judaism (after 1940)

As already indicated, since at least the year 1940, the majority of Jews in the United States have been native born; thus we can speak of a new "American Judaism" after this date. The 1986 edition of the *American Jewish Year Book* estimates that there are 5.835 million Jews in the United States today. With a total population of 236 million, this is about 2.5% of the total American population. Tables showing the Jewish populations of each state as well as world Jewish populations are given at the end of this chapter.

Two events during this period have been of crucial significance for Jews in North America as well as in the world. The first was the Holocaust, when some six million Jews were systematically put to death under the Nazis. The second was the formation of the modern State of Israel in 1948.

A major concern of the American Jewish community in recent years is reflected in a headline from an advertisement reproduced in the *Encyclopaedia Judaica Dicennial Book: 1973–1982:* ''If you're Jewish chances are your grandchildren won't be'' (p. 593). Factors leading to the decline in the number of Jews in the U.S. include the declining birthrate among American Jews, the slowing down of immigration, and assimilation into the non-Jewish community, especially through intermarriage. Concern for the decline in the number of Jews has given rise to a change in Judaism's usual reluctance to seek converts. In a 1978 speech, Reform Rabbi Alexander Shindler said, ''I believe it is time for our movement to launch a carefully conceived Outreach program aimed at all Americans who are unchurched and who are seeking roots in religion.'' An official response to this statement said that ''Judaism is not an exclusive club of born Jews; it is a universal faith with an ancient tradition which has deep resonance for people alive today (*Dicennial Book*, p. 593).

What about American Jews and religion? While accurate statistics are very difficult to obtain, they may be considered in four groups (percentages are from the *Dicennial Book*):

It is estimated that some 53% of American Jews have *no formal membership in a synagogue*. We have seen that for many of these nonaffiliated Jews, their relationship to the Jewish people may be expressed by

. participation in Jewish organizations, including those which support Israel.

Of the remaining American Jews, about 20% are *Orthodox*. Orthodoxy is firmly established in the United States. Its status was enhanced when Orthodoxy became the official religion of the State of Israel. Within Orthodoxy, the Hasidic (literally, "pietistic") groups have been the most visible. Abraham Heschel, the distinguished theologian, writer, and civil rights advocate, was of Hasidic descent. The Lubavitcher Hasidim, with their headquarters in Brooklyn, have been popularized by the novels of Chaim Potok (*The Chosen, The Promise, My Name is Asher Lev*), and are noted for their creative efforts to win less observant Jews back to a more observant life. Hasidic Jews are also known for transmitting their faith through stories; many Americans have become acquainted with these stories through the collections of Martin Buber (*Tales of the Hasidim*) and more recently Elie Wiesel, himself a descendant of eastern European Hasidim (*Souls on Fire* and other books). Buoyed by a high birth rate and success in Israel, the Orthodox may be considered the most aggressive and self-confident group in Judaism today.

Some 30% of U.S. Jews affiliated with a synagogue are estimated to be *Reform Jews*. The Reform remain the liberal wing of American Judaism, though a tendency toward a return to more traditional practices in both worship and individual observances can be noted.

A striking feature of American Judaism in this most recent period has been the growth of the *Conservative* movement, estimated at about 50% of Jews who are affiliated with a synagogue. Our brief sketch of the history of Jews in North America indicates how this has come about: at the outset, liberal German Reform Judaism dominated the American scene. This was countered by the influx of Orthodox Jews from Eastern Europe. Out of this mixture the Conservative movement emerged, and it is now the largest of the three main branches of Judaism in the United States.

Is it possible to speak of an "American Judaism" which will now play a unique role in the world? A number of observers believe so. To quote the *Dicennial Book* again:

A tantalizing question is whether within this variety of motifs some consensus pattern of American Judaism is emerging; whether with Reform Judaism showing more conservative tendencies and Conservative Judaism relaxing the control of Orthodox norms, and with the assertion of a common ethnicity pervading community life, a civil religion for American Jews is developing, with the result that, as among American Protestants, denominational labels serve inherited organizational interests and prolong past disagreements rather than indicate live theological differences (p. 594).

Jews and Christians in North America

What does all of this mean for Christians in North America? What ought to be the attitude of Christians in the United States and Canada toward their Jewish neighbors?

In the first place, all Christians are called to work toward the eradication of all forms of anti-Semitism. Anti-Jewish comments, jokes, or slogans contribute to anti-Jewish attitudes and actions which ultimately lead down the path toward another Holocaust. There are six million reasons for Christians to continue to be on the alert for anti-Semitism and to work at building a positive attitude toward Jews and Judaism. As noted elsewhere in this book, Christ's command to "love your neighbor," which he quoted from the Hebrew Bible (Lev. 19:18; see Mark 12:31), has too often not been extended to the neighbor who is Jewish (see pp. 181-200).

Secondly, now is the time for renewed and informed conversations between Christians and Jews. These may include formal dialogues such as those which have been held since the end of World War II. These dialogues, in which experts on both Jewish and Christian sides are involved, have produced a number of helpful statements; several of these are printed in Part 7 of this book. Such encounters are deserving of support from both Christians and Jews.

But conversations with Jewish neighbors at the local level should also be encouraged. Such exchanges may take place as study groups work through a book such as this one and then visit a synagogue worship service as a part of the study program. These visits may include discussion sessions at the synagogue or sessions involving Jews and Christians in homes. Such conversations at the neighborhood level are extremely valuable, and Christians should be willing to take the initiative in arranging them. Practical help in setting up synagogue visits is available through the Anti-Defamation League (see the addresses given on pp. 269-273), or one can simply call the nearest synagogue. With a bit of energy and imagination, Christians and Jews in a community can get to know one another in a way that is mutually beneficial.

ESTIMATED JEWISH POPULATION, BY CONTINENTS AND MAJOR GEOGRAPHICAL REGIONS, 1982 AND 1984

Region	1982 Original	1982 Revised Abs. Nos.	1982 Revised %	1984 Abs. Nos.	1984 %	% change 1982-1984
Diaspora	9,614,300	9,594,300	74.1	9,491,600	73.2	-1.1
Israel	3,374,300	3,349,600	25.9	3,471,700	26.8	+3.6
World	12,988,600	12,943,900	100.0	12,963,300	100.0	+0.2
America, Total	6,477,700	6,477,600	50.1	6,469,000	49.9	-1.3
North[a]	6,013,000	6,015,000	46.5	6,015,000	46.4	—
Central	46,800	46,800	0.4	47,300	0.4	+1.1
South	417,900	415,800	3.2	406,700	3.1	-2.2
Europe, Total	2,842,700	2,825,100	21.8	2,758,600	21.3	-2.6
West	1,070,900	1,053,300	8.1	1,048,900	8.1	-1.0
East & Balkans[b]	1,771,800	1,771,800	13.7	1,709,700	13.2	-3.5
Asia, Total	3,417,200	3,392,500	26.2	3,509,300	27.1	+3.4
Israel	3,374,300	3,349,600	25.9	3,471,700	26.8	+3.6
Rest[b]	42,900	42,900	0.3	37,600	0.3	-12.4
Africa, Total	172,000	169,700	1.3	147,400	1.1	-13.3
North	21,250	19,950	0.2	16,700	0.1	-17.5
South	120,250	119,250	0.9	119,100	0.9	-0.1
Rest[c]	30,500	30,500	0.2	11,600	0.1	-62.0
Oceania	79,000	79,000	0.6	79,000	0.6	—

[a]U.S.A. and Canada.
[b]The Asian territories of USSR and Turkey are included in ''East Europe and Balkans.''
[c]Including Ethiopia.

COUNTRIES WITH LARGEST JEWISH POPULATIONS (100,000 JEWS AND ABOVE), 1984

Rank	Country	Jewish Population	% of Total Jewish Population In the Diaspora %	Cum. %	In the World %	Cum. %
1	United States	5,705,000	60.1	60.1	44.0	44.0
2	Israel	3,471,700	—	—	26.8	70.8
3	Soviet Union	1,575,000	16.6	76.7	12.1	82.9
4	France	530,000	5.6	82.3	4.1	87.0
5	Great Britain	330,000	3.5	85.8	2.5	89.5
6	Canada	310,000	3.3	89.1	2.4	91.9
7	Argentina	228,000	2.4	91.5	1.8	93.7
8	South Africa	118,000	1.2	92.7	0.9	94.6
9	Brazil	100,000	1.0	93.7	0.8	95.4

JEWISH POPULATION IN THE UNITED STATES, 1985

State	Estimated Jewish Population	Total Population*	Estimated Jewish Percent of Total
Alabama	9,400	3,990,000	0.2
Alaska	960	500,000	0.2
Arizona	68,285	3,053,000	2.2
Arkansas	2,975	2,349,000	0.1
California	793,065	25,622,000	3.1
Colorado	48,565	3,178,000	1.5
Connecticut	105,400	3,154,000	3.3
Delaware	9,500	613,000	1.6
District of Columbia	24,285	622,823	3.9
Florida	570,320	10,976,000	5.2
Georgia	58,570	5,837,000	1.0
Hawaii	5,550	1,039,000	0.5
Idaho	505	1,001,000	0.1
Illinois	262,710	11,511,000	2.3
Indiana	21,335	5,498,000	0.4
Iowa	5,570	2,910,000	0.2
Kansas	11,430	2,438,000	0.5
Kentucky	12,775	3,723,000	0.3
Louisiana	17,405	4,462,000	0.4
Maine	9,350	1,156,000	0.8
Maryland	199,415	4,439,000	4.5
Massachusetts	249,370	5,798,000	4.3
Michigan	86,125	9,075,000	0.9
Minnesota	32,240	4,162,000	0.8
Mississippi	3,130	2,598,000	0.1
Missouri	64,690	5,008,000	1.3
Montana	645	824,000	0.1
Nebraska	7,865	1,606,000	0.5
Nevada	18,200	911,000	2.0
New Hampshire	5,980	977,000	0.6
New Jersey	430,570	7,515,000	5.7
New Mexico	5,155	1,424,000	0.4
New York	1,915,145	17,735,000	10.8
North Carolina	14,990	6,165,000	0.2
North Dakota	1,085	686,000	0.2
Ohio	138,935	10,752,000	1.3
Oklahoma	6,885	3,298,000	0.2
Oregon	11,050	2,674,000	0.4
Pennsylvania	353,045	11,901,000	3.0
Rhode Island	22,000	962,000	2.3

South Carolina	8,095	3,300,000	0.2
South Dakota	635	706,000	0.1
Tennessee	19,445	4,717,000	0.4
Texas	78,655	15,989,000	0.5
Utah	2,850	1,652,000	0.2
Vermont	2,465	530,000	0.5
Virginia	60,185	5,636,000	1.1
Washington	22,085	4,149,000	0.5
West Virginia	4,265	1,952,000	0.2
Wisconsin	31,190	4,766,000	0.7
Wyoming	310	511,000	0.1
U.S. TOTAL	**5,834,655	236,031,000	2.5

N.B. Details may not add to totals because of rounding.

*Resident population, July 1, 1984, provisional. (Source: *Provisional Estimates of the Population of Counties: July 1984,* Bureau of the Census, series P-26, No. 84-52-C, March 1985.)

**Exclusive of Puerto Rico and the Virgin Islands, which previously reported Jewish populations of 1,800 and 510, respectively.

Source: *American Jewish Year Book: A Record of Events and Trends in American and World Jewish Life,* American Jewish Committee and Jewish Publication Society of America, 1986.

2

An Outline of Jewish History

In the preceding chapter we have traced the story of the Jews in North America. But where did these people originate? What has been their history? The brief historical sketch that follows will focus on these questions and will provide the historical framework for the materials in the chapters that follow.

The Beginnings

In the period known as the Early Bronze Age (c. 3200–1500 B.C.), the ancestors of Abraham and Sarah lived in Mesopotamia. Sometime in the Middle Bronze Age (c. 2000–1500 B.C.), Abraham and his family moved to Canaan, but did not settle there permanently. At that time the territory along the Mediterranean coast was under Egyptian control, and other peoples lived inland, among them the Hittites in Asia Minor. Toward the end of this period, independent of events in Canaan, came the stay in Egypt, the Exodus under the leadership of Moses, and the events at Mount Sinai.

The Settlement of the Land

Not until the end of the Late Bronze Age (c. 1500–1200 B.C.) did nomadic tribes, among them Israelites, settle in the mountainous areas of Palestine. The "judges," Israel's leaders in the years after 1200 B.C., were the first to give temporary political stability to the loosely-organized tribal league of the Israelites. The monarchy under Saul brought about a more permanent structure.

The Formation of the State

In about the year 1000 B.C., under the leadership of King David (c. 1000–961 B.C.), the Israelites succeeded in establishing a state in what later became Syro-Palestinian territory. This state, with Jerusalem as its capital, united the tribes living in the northern and southern parts of the land. Solomon held the nation together during his administration (c. 961-922 B.C.), but after his death it quickly split into the northern kingdom ("Israel") and the southern kingdom ("Judah"). The two nations were periodically at war with each other, until Assyria conquered the northern kingdom in 721 B.C.

The Babylonian Captivity

In the years after the fall of Israel, Judah was subject to the rule of various superpowers and was involved in wars with the smaller nations surrounding it. Judah experienced yet another time of political, social, and religious flowering under Josiah (640–609 B.C.). This came to an end in the year 587 B.C., when the Babylonians conquered Jerusalem and destroyed the temple. The people who had the most economic and religious influence were deported to Babylon. Living in separate colonies as a minority in the midst of a population which had religious beliefs quite different from their own, these Jews held strongly to their religious traditions. After the loss of the temple, which was their religious center, such things as circumcision, the Sabbath rest, and dietary laws took on new meaning. A new form of community worship developed which was not dependent on special holy places and which could take place anywhere.

The Return

After the fall of the Babylonian empire, Cyrus the Persian came to power. With his more open policy toward the people under his control, he made possible the return of the Jews to Jerusalem (538–530 B.C.). These Jews who returned expended great efforts to rebuild the city walls and the temple, which was dedicated in 515 B.C. The separation of the Jews from the Samaritans who were living in the former territory of the northern kingdom took place during this time.

Under Hellenistic Influence

The conquests of Alexander the Great (336-323 B.C.) set in motion a wave of hellenistic (Greek) influence which rolled over the entire Near East and did not let up even after the empire broke into smaller kingdoms. The Jews in the Diaspora (those living outside Israel) were especially affected: they took up the common Greek language which was used throughout the hellenistic empire and translated the Hebrew Scriptures into it. At first, the Jews in Judah were allowed to regulate their own religious affairs under the leadership of their high priest. But then the hellenistic ruler of Syria-Palestine carried out a full program of imposing Greek culture on the population, with the forced removal of the high priest, the plundering of the temple treasury, the compulsory introduction of hellenistic state religion, and the prohibition of the ancient Jewish traditions. Some of the Jews fiercely resisted these changes.

The Time of the Maccabees

In the years 166–160 B.C., Judas Maccabeus led the Jewish fight against the hellenistic Syrians. In 164 B.C. Judas succeeded in capturing Jerusalem. His first task was the rededication of the temple. After his death, Jews willing to fight for their faith continued the resistance under the leadership of Judas's brothers. Under the high priest Simon, Judah once again won its independence for a short time. Simon founded the dynasty of the Maccabees or Hasmoneans. His sons even succeeded in expanding the territory of the state, gaining control of Samaria in the north and Idumea in the south.

Three main Jewish groups which marked the religious life of the people in the land gradually developed out of the political struggles of that period: the Pharisees, who advocated strict obedience to the Torah (the prescriptions contained in the first five books of the Bible) and established numerous regulations so that the prescriptions of the Torah could be observed; the Essenes, deeply influenced by strong apocalyptic and messianic expectations, who had their own religious community at Qumran; and the Sadducees, the party of the priests and of members of well-to-do families, who strove for the political and religious influence of their group.

Under Roman Rule

Pompey's conquest of Jerusalem in 63 B.C. meant the end of the Maccabean high priestly kingdom and a growing dependence of all Jewish leaders upon Rome. Herod the Great, named as king over Judah by the Romans in 40 B.C., made special efforts to gain the favor of Rome. But as an upstart from Idumea and because of his cruel policies, he had no support among his own people. Those who held the real power in the land were the Roman procurators, who were entrusted with governing the provinces. During the administration of Pontius Pilate (A.D. 26–36), Jesus of Nazareth preached and was crucified. In A.D. 66 the Jews rebelled against Rome. After a long siege the Roman general Titus conquered Jerusalem in A.D. 70, destroyed the city and the temple, and thereby took away the geographical and religious center of the Jews. Further rebellions against the Romans by Jews in the Diaspora and under the leadership of Bar Kochba in the land itself (A.D. 132–135) did not alter the balance of political power. Jerusalem became a Roman colony and Jews were not allowed to enter the city.

Scattered among the Nations

During the second and third centuries A.D., Jews were living in Palestine and also scattered throughout the entire Roman Empire. Beginning in the fourth century, the increasingly strong Christian influence on the Roman Empire resulted in oppression of Jews. Anti-Jewish laws multiplied, and confrontations between Christianity and Judaism became more and more intense. Under Islam, which spread out further and further from the Near East beginning in the seventh century, Jews were tolerated as a minority, and Babylonian and North African Judaism were able to maintain themselves. In Spain from 900–1140, under Islamic domination, Judaism even flourished. Jews in France also lived without interference for a long time, until the Crusades, when Jews were persecuted and driven out of country after country throughout Western Europe.

The fate of Jews in Eastern and Western Europe always depended on the favor or disfavor of the ruler in whose land they lived. It was not until the 19th century that the effects of the French Revolution (1789) brought about a gradual improvement of their legal and social situation, at least in Western Europe. In Eastern Europe, on the other hand, Jews did not gain equal rights, but were again and again the victims of cruel persecutions and pogroms.

Catastrophe and New Beginning

At the same time that Jews were being oppressed in Eastern Europe in the 19th century, the first ideas of modern Jewish nationalism developed. Beginning in 1882, several waves of emigrant Jews from Czarist Russia settled in the land of their ancestors. Under the pressure of modern anti-Semitism (hatred of Jews), the ideas of Zionism also gained ground in Western Europe (see the excerpt from the Balfour Declaration, p. 62).

After National Socialism gained power in Germany in the 1930s, Jews began to flee from areas under German control into the whole world. In the years up to 1945, some six million European Jews who were not able to escape the horrors of the Nazi regime were murdered. The proclamation announcing the birth of the independent State of Israel in 1948 marked a new beginning in the history of the Jews (see the excerpt from Israel's Declaration of Independence on pp. 48-50).

PART TWO

ISRAEL—
PEOPLE,
PEOPLE OF GOD,
COUNTRY, AND LAND

3

Israel: Not Just a Country

Nowadays we come across the word *Israel* most often as the name of a country: the State of Israel. But because the word also has other meanings, there are often misunderstandings. Therefore some explanation is needed.

Israel: A State

Israel was officially declared a state on May 14, 1948, after the November 1947 decision of the United Nations to divide Palestine into Jewish and Arab sectors. This state has been established in the land in which the history of God's people Israel took place, as that history is told in the Old Testament. Even though for many centuries the majority of Jews have had to live outside the land, their attachment to Mount Zion in Jerusalem, to the land of their ancestors, and to those Jews living there has remained strong.

The initial move toward founding the State of Israel came at the end of the 19th century with Zionism, whose most famous champion was Theodor Herzl (1860–1904). The goal of this movement was the founding of a separate Jewish state in Palestine, the ancestral homeland. Because of anti-Semitism and persecution in Europe, and the Nazi policy of extermination of Jews, the establishment of the state became a matter of life or death for Judaism.

The State of Israel is organized in the form of a parliamentary democracy. Its citizens include not only Jews, but also Christian and Muslim Arabs and others who have lived in the land for centuries. But because this country still regards itself to a great degree as a "Jewish state," its formation has led to tensions which have not been resolved to this day. At issue is the displacement of Palestinians who lived in the land, resulting from conflicts over the past decades.

The State of Israel cannot be equated with the Jewish people, because only about 3½ million of the approximately 13 million Jews in the world live there.

Israel: A People

Israel is also the Old Testament name of the people of God. This people traces its ancestry from the patriarch Jacob (Genesis 25) who received the name Israel directly from God (Genesis 32). According to the biblical witness, Israel was made up of 12 tribes which bore the names of Jacob's sons (Exodus 1). These people were bound together by the Hebrew language, but also by their confession of belief in the one God who had led them out of bondage in Egypt into the promised land, had made a covenant with them at Sinai and had given them the Torah (the first five books of the Bible) to govern their lives.

The kingdom that Saul and David founded, made up of the whole people of Israel, split after the death of Solomon (about 922 B.C.). From that point on, only the northern part carried the name of Israel, while the southern part named itself after the tribe of Judah. After the fall of the northern kingdom (Israel) to the Assyrians (722–721 B.C.), only the southern kingdom remained, with Jerusalem as its capital. After that time the term *Jews* (that is, citizens of Judah) instead of *Israelites* became the usual designation for these people. Since the destruction of Jerusalem by the Babylonians (587 B.C.), and especially after the onslaughts by the Romans (A.D. 70 and 135), the Jews have lived as both a religious and an ethnic minority in the midst of other nations. They are known as Jews and refer to themselves by that name. Nevertheless, they continue to regard themselves as belonging to God's people Israel, and also use that name, especially in religious contexts. The New Testament also frequently calls the Jewish people "Israel."

Israel: A Community

The form of Jewish synagogue worship developed during the Babylonian exile in the sixth century B.C., and religious observances in the home grew out of the synagogue services. Scripture reading and prayer were central to synagogue worship. Since the time of the destruction of the Jerusalem temple in A.D. 70, Jews have been able to have community worship only in synagogues. Therefore *Israel* also came to designate the community assembled in a synagogue.

Israel and the Church

One more use of the term *Israel* should also be mentioned here. In the New Testament, the name *Israel* was also used by the community of those who believed in Jesus. According to the witness of the New Testament and of Christianity, Jesus Christ is the promised Messiah of Israel and the Savior of the entire world. He assembles his new people Israel out of both Jews and Gentiles. In this sense the church also applies the term *Israel* to itself. However, the church has no right to forget or to despise those Jews who call themselves "Israel" (see Romans 9–11). The story of how Christians have again and again caused much suffering to come upon Jews belongs to the dark pages of the history of the church. For all Christians, this story is a call to repentance.

So both Jews and Christians call themselves "Israel," though in different ways. This has created a tension between the two communities that has still not been resolved. According to Jewish teaching, if a Jew comes to faith in Jesus Christ, that person parts company with the people of Israel. To the person who makes such a decision, however, faith in Jesus as the Messiah appears to be the fulfillment of his or her Jewish identity.

Despite the burdens of the past and the unresolved tensions of the present, Christians and Jews today are once again becoming acquainted with one another. This is a sign of hope.

Excerpt from The Israel Declaration of Independence

On May 15, 1948, in the name of the People's Council meeting in Tel-Aviv, David Ben Gurion proclaimed the existence of the State of Israel. Among other things, Israel's Declaration of Independence says the following:

Eretz [Hebrew, "the land of"] Israel was the birthplace of the Jewish people. Here their spiritual, religious and political identity was shaped. Here they first attained to statehood, created cultural values of national and universal significance and gave to the world the eternal Book of Books.

After being forcibly exiled from their land, the people kept faith with it throughout their Dispersion and never ceased to pray and hope for their return to it and for the restoration in it of their political freedom. . . .

The catastrophe which recently befell the Jewish people—the massacre of millions of Jews in Europe—was another clear demonstration of the urgency of solving the problem of its homelessness by re-establishing in Eretz-Israel the Jewish State, which would open the gates of the homeland wide to every Jew and confer upon the Jewish people the status of a fully-privileged member of the comity of nations. . . .

Accordingly we, members of the People's Council, representatives of the Jewish community of Eretz-Israel and of the Zionist movement, are here assembled on the day of the termination of the British Mandate over Eretz-Israel and, by virtue of our natural and historic right and on the strength of the resolution of the United Nations General Assembly, hereby declare the establishment of a Jewish State in Eretz-Israel, to be known as the State of Israel.

The State of Israel will be open for Jewish immigration and for the Ingathering of the Exiles; it will foster the development of the country for the benefit of all inhabitants; it will be based on freedom, justice and peace as envisaged by the prophets of Israel; it will ensure complete equality of social and political rights to all its inhabitants irrespective of religion, race or sex; it will guarantee freedom of religion, conscience, language, education and culture; it will safeguard the Holy Places of all religions; and it will be faithful to the principles of the Charter of the United Nations . . . .

We appeal—in the very midst of the onslaught launched against us now for months—to the Arab inhabitants of the State of Israel to preserve peace and participate in the up-building of the State on the basis of full and equal citizenship and due representation in all its provisional and permanent institutions.

We extend our hand to all neighbouring states and their peoples in an offer of peace and good neighbourliness, and appeal to them to establish bonds of cooperation and mutual help with the sovereign Jewish people settled in its own land. The State of Israel is prepared to do its share in common effort for the advancement of the entire Middle East.

Excerpt from the Law of Return

This law, passed on July 5, 1950, states, among other things, that:

1. Every Jew has the right to emigrate to the country.
3a. A Jew who comes to Israel and after his arrival expresses a desire to settle there may, while in Israel, obtain an immigrant certificate.

An amendment added in 1970, "for the first time, defines the word 'Jew,' for purposes of the Law of Return, as a person born to a Jewish mother, or who has been converted to Judaism, and who has not adopted any other faith."

(*Readings in Modern Jewish History* by Eliezer L. Ehrmann, pp. 293-294; *Encyclopaedia Judaica Decennial Book: 1973-1982*, p. 361.)

4

The Land of Israel

Whoever is concerned with Israel today—with the Jewish people, their faith, or the State of Israel—quickly discovers the importance of the land. Jewish faith is nourished by the triad of Bible, people, and land. According to that faith, these three belong together. Christians, too, have certain conceptions and expectations which are tied to the land and to the state which has been established there.

In order to make a judgment about the present situation in the Middle East, or to understand Judaism at all, it is important to look first at the biblical witness about the land, a witness which is common to both Jews and Christians.

Promised Land

According to the testimony of the stories about the patriarchs and Moses in Genesis and Exodus, God promised the land of Canaan to the people of Israel. God pledged to the patriarchs Abraham, Isaac, and Jacob that he would give the land to them and their descendants as the "promised land" (Genesis 12; 26; 28). When Israel was in bondage in Egypt, God promised they would return to the land where their ancestors had lived (see Exodus 3, for example). These promises found their initial fulfillment after the deliverance from Egypt, in the conquest of the land under the leadership of Joshua: "Not one of all the good promises which the Lord had made to the house of Israel had failed; all came to pass" (Josh. 21:45).

The promises about the land are almost always bound together with other promises, such as the promise of descendants, of being a blessing for the nations, and of a covenant between God and God's people.

So the land was associated with the faith of the people of God from the beginning and especially with their obedience and their faithfulness to the covenant. The land was God's gift to God's people, but it was never Israel's irrevocable possession to be used however they wished. Rather, it was to be managed by the people in conformity with the will of the God who had given it.

Entrusted Land

The connection between people, land, and faith in the one God therefore did not exist from the beginning. It came about through the saving acts of God in history. God is not tied to a land, but is Lord of the entire world; God chose this people, delivered them, made a covenant with them at Sinai, and gave them this land. Since that time, God, people, and land have belonged together.

According to the Old Testament, the historical development of this connection has been under the direction of Israel's God. Even so, the borders of the land called "Canaan" were never clearly established for Israel. Also, a distinction was made between the concept of the land as a political entity and as land which can be farmed.

The designation "land of Israel" seldom occurs in the Bible; more often the land is spoken of as an "allotment" and "inheritance," thereby stressing the fact that the land is and remains God's gift. This idea is also preserved in Israelite land law (the key passage is Lev. 25:23) and in the institution of the sabbatical year, according to which the land is to be left uncultivated every seventh year (Leviticus 25). The land was not given to the people for exploitation, but was entrusted to them for care.

Lost Land

Because of Israel's failure to measure up to the expectations of God's will, the prophets had to announce the coming judgment and to threaten the loss of the land along with it. Israel had proved to be unworthy of the gift of the land because they had not lived according to God's commandments as God's people (see Amos 7:7-10; Mic. 2:1-5; Isa. 1:19; 5:1-10).

The removal of the most influential class of the people from the land during the Babylonian exile (587–538 B.C.) brought a new dimension to the meaning of the land for Israel's faith. The people hoped and prayed for the recovery and reclaiming of the land on the basis of God's mercy (Jeremiah; Ezekiel; Lamentations). That mercy was promised to the people anew (Isaiah 40–55): God would return to Zion along with God's own people. This hope was closely tied up with the longing for the reconstruction of the temple and the reestablishment of the kingdom of David, which soon became the central core of messianic expectation. The renewed gift of the land then called for a new obedience and a new covenant (Jer. 31:31).

In the later writings of the Old Testament, the land is completely bound up with the final fulfillment of God's promises, the new creation and the new Jerusalem. It will be God's ultimate gift to the new people of God in the end time.

In view of these expressions of hope on the one side and the reality of the present-day State of Israel on the other, it will be necessary to ask to what degree we can speak of these promises as having been fulfilled.

Israel's Land

Since ancient times the Jews have called the land *Eretz Israel,* "the land of Israel." But since the 6th century B.C. there have also been Jews living outside the land, in the Diaspora (the dispersion or scattering of the Jews throughout the world). After the catastrophe of the two unsuccessful revolts against the Romans in the years A.D. 70 and 135, Jews were even forbidden to live in the land, in Judea. The ancient name of the land was taken away and the Roman designation *Palestine* was given to it. Since that time the majority of the Jewish people have lived in the Diaspora—at present, 9½ million out of 13 million Jews.

The Jews have shown that despite separation from the land, a life in fellowship with God is possible, and they have created new forms for Jewish life. However, they have never ceased to demonstrate their ties to the land; today this often means financial contributions to the State of Israel. Many Jews living outside the land want to be buried in Israel. The longing for Zion is expressed in many prayers and customs (for example, in the wish at the celebration of Passover, " . . . next year in Jerusalem"). Thus it is of great importance for Jewish self-understanding and for Jews all over the world (even if they themselves never emigrate to Israel) that this land is once again populated by Jews.

Holy Land

Christians often speak of the land of Israel as the "Holy Land" because the history of the ancient people of God and especially the saving events connected with Jesus Christ took place there. The Gospels testify to the relationship of Jesus and his disciples to this land. In the New Testament, Jerusalem plays a special role. References to the Old Testament recall the promises to Israel which continue to be valid for Israel (see Acts 7:2-5; Heb. 11:8-16; Rom. 9:4; but see also Gal. 3:16). But since the New Testament claims that all the promises of the Old Testament are related to Jesus Christ and fulfilled in him, the Old Testament promises of the land are not renewed in the New Testament for Christians. Although the New Testament sees the Jewish response to Jesus Christ as critical for the destinies of both the land and the people (Matt. 23:37—25:46), it never speaks of an ultimate loss of the land and an end to Israel's existence.

For Christians, a knowledge of the land as well as an encounter with the people who live in it can help in gaining a deeper understanding of the Bible. The land and the locations mentioned in the Bible can be special and memorable places, but they can never claim a special honor for themselves (John 4). Because "holy places" of Christianity, Judaism, and Islam are found in the land of the Bible, all involved are obligated to search for political solutions which take these religious connections into consideration.

Many Christians ask whether the recovery of the land by the Jewish people in the establishment of the State of Israel can be understood as the fulfillment of biblical promises. In considering this issue, the New

Testament's restraint in speaking of the land's significance for the faith should be observed. For Jews, however, the land itself is a gift of salvation and as such has meaning for salvation. That which ties Jews and Christians together in regard to the land is the fact that God has revealed himself in historical saving acts which have taken place in it.

Excerpt from The Kuzari *by the poet* Judah Halevi

Judah ben Samuel Halevi (lived in Spain, 1075-1141) was also called the "Zionist of the Middle Ages" because in his poetry he again and again described a return to the land in which the Torah could be put into practice in the fullest sense. One of his dialogs says:

They [the rabbis] further say: It is better to dwell in the Holy Land, even in a town mostly inhabited by heathens, than abroad in a town chiefly peopled by Israelites; for he who dwells in the Holy Land is compared to him who has a God, whilst he who dwells abroad is compared to him who has not God. . . . Another saying is: To be buried in Palestine is as if buried beneath the altar. They praise him who is in the land more than him who is carried there dead. This is expressed thus: He who embraces it when alive is not like him who does so after his death. . . . Further, the atmosphere of the Holy Land makes wise. They expressed their love of the land as follows: He who walks four yards in the land is assured of happiness in the world to come, R. Zera said to a heathen who criticized his foolhardiness in crossing a river without waiting to reach a ford, in his eagerness to enter the land: How can the place which Moses and Aaron could not reach, be reached by me?

(Judah Halevi, *The Kuzari: An Argument for the Faith of Israel,* Schocken, 1964.)

5

Zionism

The word *Zionism* has been in the spotlight of world affairs recently, especially since the declaration of the General Assembly of the United Nations in the fall of 1975 that Zionism is "a form of racism." This reproach has affected not only Jews within and outside of Israel, but also Christians, many of whom see the return of the Jews to their ancient homeland as a sign of God's faithfulness to his people.

In this situation Christians must also ask: What, really, is Zionism?

Zion

Zion is a mountain in Jerusalem. It became especially important because King David made Jerusalem his capital city and the center for the people of Israel. As time went on, the name *Zion* called to mind the temple, all of Jerusalem, and the entire people in the land of the patriarchs.

In the Babylonian exile after the first destruction of Jerusalem (587 B.C.), a longing to return to God's promised land awakened among the deported Jews. The tie to the land of Israel was never broken for the Jews who had been scattered throughout the Mediterranean world since ancient times (the Diaspora); this was a part of their faith. The longing for Zion became especially strong after A.D. 70 and 135; at each of these times it appeared that the land would be lost forever. But there have always been Jews living in the land, as individuals or in communities. Those living outside the land remembered the land of their ancestors in their daily prayers. Journeys to the land were considered pilgrimages, and many wished at least to be buried there. Modern Zionism links up with this ancient longing for Zion.

Zionism

Beginning in the early 1800s, the Jews in many parts of Europe gradually received full rights as citizens (emancipation). At that time many gave up their Jewish tradition, either fully or partially, in order to fit into European culture and society. This process is referred to as "assimilation." Many Jews understood their Judaism as a religion which was not tied to any particular land. This development came to a halt after 1870, when a new form of anti-Semitism emerged; in Eastern Europe there were even bloody persecutions (pogroms).

At that time many Jews became conscious of their own lack of a land and of a tie to the land of their ancestors. In 1896 the Vienna journalist Theodor Herzl wrote the book *The Jewish State,* which became the platform for a new political movement named "Zionism." Its goal was to help Jews gain a sense of self-respect as an independent people as well as to win the respect of non-Jews. A homeland for the Jews in the land of Israel in which their rights as a people were guaranteed would make all this possible. At first, religious and biblical ideas played a small role in the Zionist movement; it reflected the spirit of the times, during which many peoples pressed for national independence and many groups sought social justice.

After 1882, groups of Jews began settling in regions of Palestine which had been for the most part unoccupied. The declaration of the British foreign minister

Balfour in 1917 seemed to guarantee the rights of the Jews in Palestine to have that land as a national homeland. After this declaration, the tempo of Jewish settlement in Palestine picked up. Yet at the same time, Great Britain had also promised the Arabs sovereignty over the entire Middle East.

During the period of the Nazi persecutions, many Jews fled to the land of their ancestors. Increasing tensions during the time when the land was under British administration led to the November 1947 decision of the United Nations to divide the land into Jewish and Arab sectors. When the power of the British mandate over Palestine was withdrawn, the existence of the State of Israel was declared on May 14, 1948, and it was recognized as a nation by the majority of the member states of the United Nations. The goal of the Zionists appeared to have been reached.

Anti-Zionism

From the time of its founding, the State of Israel has been in conflict with its Arab neighbors. Zionism strove for peaceful coexistence and did not wish to drive the Arabs out of their ancestral homes. However, while Zionism was developing among the Jews, a national movement also came into being among the Arabs; they saw themselves as the legitimate owners of the entire land. The result of these opposing viewpoints was conflict and much suffering among innocent people on both sides, brought about by the partisan involvements of the superpowers as well as by political mistakes made by the participants. The conflict remains unresolved to this day, despite many proposed solutions, including those from the United Nations.

Except for Egypt, which signed a peace treaty with Israel in 1979 as a result of the Camp David conversations, Israel's Arab neighbors have continued to deny recognition to Israel as a nation and have not recognized its borders; the right of Israel to exist as a nation thus remains disputed. Over the years, Israel has become less and less willing to come to an agreement or to compromise with the Arabs; for Israel, the demonstration of military strength has appeared to be the only way out of its dilemma. On the Arab side, anti-Israeli sentiment came to a climax in the cry, "Drive them into the sea!" Since the Six-day War in June 1967, Israel has been an occupying power over the Arabs living in the West Bank area (the west bank of the Jordan River); this has made a peaceful agreement with the Arabs all the more difficult.

The Zionist movement's continuing appeal to support the State of Israel, a country endangered by four wars and innumerable acts of terrorism, has found a hearing with Jews throughout the world. Zionism has thus gained new significance as it has captured the attention of the great majority of Jews.

In recent times, many enemies of the Jews have rallied under the banner of anti-Zionism. They maintain that their efforts are directed only against the policies of the State of Israel, not against Jews as individuals. However, it is all too easy for the old, anti-Semitic ideology to lurk behind this movement. Some persons who hate Jews hide behind the excuse that they are only opposed to Zionism. This kind of hatred does not shy away from discrimination, slander, and even plans for destroying the Jews.

Racism?

On November 10, 1975, prompted by the Arab states and with the support of the Eastern Block and many non-European member states, the General Assembly of the United Nations declared Zionism to be "a form of racism."

History shows that Zionism arose as a response to the racist attacks of others. In view of what the Jewish people have gone through in the past, extreme reserve in making such reproaches is advisable—despite many controversial actions on the part of Israel as an occupying power. It is difficult to understand that precisely those nations that do not allow basic human rights to the Jews or to the other national and religious minorities who live among them are the ones who have made charges against Israel.

Many believe that the decision of the United Nations was a conscious attack on the right of the State of Israel to exist and also an attack against the Jews in general. The blanket disparagement of Zionism and, by implication, Israel, undermines those who speak up for understanding and compromise, from either the Arab or the Jewish side; it does not make for peace, but sows new seeds of hatred.

The task for Christians is to accompany the Jews along their way in critical solidarity. The United Nations' charge of racism ought to be emphatically opposed. But it also needs to be remembered that equal rights for all citizens of the State of Israel—regardless of their nationality or religion—remains one of the unresolved problems of the young nation, even though this was not originally a problem for Zionism.

Excerpt from Theodor Herzl, The Jewish State, 1896

No human being is wealthy or powerful enough to transplant a nation from one habitation to another. An idea alone can compass that; and this idea of a State may have the requisite power to do so. The Jews have dreamt their kingly dream all through the long nights of their history. "Next year in Jerusalem" is our old phrase. It is now a question of showing that the dream can be converted into a living reality.

(*The Jewish State: An Attempt at a Modern Solution of the Jewish Question* by Theodor Herzl, H. Pordes, 1967, pp. 19-20.)

Excerpt from the Balfour Declaration of November 2, 1917

The British foreign secretary, Arthur James Balfour, sent a declaration to the "English Zionist Federation" in which the following was said:

His Majesty's government view with favour the establishment in Palestine of a national home for the Jewish people, and will use their best endeavours to facilitate the achievement of this object, it being clearly understood that nothing shall be done which may prejudice the civil and religious rights of existing non-Jewish communities in Palestine, or the rights and political status enjoyed by Jews in any other country.

6

Jerusalem

The land of the Bible is filled with powerful tensions which have their origins in the distant past. Several factors have contributed to these tensions: the variety of historical experiences and political traditions of the inhabitants of the land, the various civilizations which meet here, and the unique geographical situation. An important factor in these tensions is the fact that three world religions are related to this land.

The conflicting religious claims have their focal point in the city of Jerusalem. Since biblical times, Jerusalem has been the religious center of Judaism. For Christians—especially the Eastern Orthodox Church—it is the city of the "holy places." Most European church buildings are "oriented" toward Jerusalem (that is, toward the east), the site of the crucifixion and resurrection of Jesus Christ. Jerusalem is also a holy city for the world of Islam; in Arabic it is simply called Al-Quds (the holy). The degree to which the hopes of these three religions are directed toward this place is evident as one looks at the three large cemeteries in the Kidron Valley: the Jewish cemetery on the west side of the Mount of Olives, the Muslim cemetery across from it, and the Christian cemetery in the valley below.

The special significance which Jerusalem has for Judaism, Christianity, and Islam is evident from three striking structures: the remains of the temple, the Church of the Holy Sepulchre, and the Dome of the Rock.

A young boy, wearing a prayer shawl, carries the Torah with the help of a friend, after his Bar Mitzvah at Jerusalem's Western Wall.

The Western ("Wailing") Wall of the Temple Area: Holy Place for Jews

After King David had conquered the Canaanite city of Jerusalem and had made it the capital of his kingdom, his son Solomon built the temple there, on a rocky area on Mount Moriah, almost 1000 years before Christ.

This temple became the central sanctuary—later the only sanctuary—where offerings could be made. In other words, the temple was the center for Jewish faith. Jews from everywhere came to the temple for the three pilgrimage festivals (see Deut. 16:16). Destroyed by the Babylonians in 587 B.C., the temple was rebuilt a few generations later. Shortly before the time of Jesus, Herod the Great expanded the temple in grand fashion. This temple was also reduced to ashes and rubble when the Romans conquered Jerusalem in A.D. 70; only the supporting walls remained standing. After the suppression of a second Jewish revolt (A.D. 135), a Roman temple was erected in its place and Jerusalem was made a Roman city, to which Jews had no access for a long time.

The significance of the temple for Jerusalem, however, had by no means come to an end. To be sure, the temple was never again rebuilt—to this day there are no plans to do so. After the temple's destruction, prayer and good works took the place of sacrifices. But the orientation toward Jerusalem and Mount Zion has remained without change. The greeting at the end of the Passover meal goes, " . . . next year in Jerusalem!" In legend and in prayer, Jerusalem remains the object of devotion and hope: "Bring our exiled ones from the ends of the earth back to Jerusalem!" The Western Wall of the temple, at the foot of the temple mountain, known among Christians as the "Wailing Wall," has special meaning for Jewish piety. Jews faithful to their tradition who did not and could not set foot on the temple mountain itself prayed at this place, which was at one time a narrow street in front of the temple's massive stonework. From 1948 to 1967 Jews were denied access to the Western Wall. Since 1967 a spacious place for prayer has been constructed—accessible to Christians also—where Jews from all over the world appear, especially on festival days and for Bar Mitzvah celebrations. No other place gives such dramatic evidence of the central significance of Jerusalem for Judaism.

The Church of the Holy Sepulchre: Holy Place for Christians

The stone dome of the Church of the Holy Sepulchre rises up in the middle of Jerusalem's Old City. On its premises, according to tradition, are the sites of the burial and resurrection of Jesus Christ as well as Golgotha, the place of the crucifixion. This part of the city was also destroyed by the Romans in the Jewish revolts, and a pagan temple was built there. The Byzantine Queen Helena, the mother of Constantine, had the first Church of the Sepulchre built just after A.D. 300. In the course of the centuries it has often been destroyed, rebuilt, expanded, and changed. After difficult struggles, the various Christian churches of the Mediterranean world have established their claims to parts of the building; they were trying to establish the closest possible connection with the place where Jesus died and rose from the dead.

The dome of the Church of the Holy Sepulchre in Jerusalem.

Although Protestant Christians have a difficult time understanding this struggle for a share of the holy places, they also have a special affection for Jerusalem. Proof of this is found in the many Christian pilgrims who have streamed to the "Holy Land" and especially to Jerusalem for centuries in order to follow in the footsteps of Jesus. The countless Christian establishments and institutes in Jerusalem also testify to the special significance Jerusalem has for Christians of all confessions.

The Dome of the Rock: Holy Place for Muslims

The golden dome of the Dome of the Rock, which may be seen from a great distance, rises out of the area of what was once the Herodian temple. Near it gleams the smaller, silver dome of the Mosque of Aksa. These are reminders that next to Mecca and Medina, Jerusalem has the greatest meaning for Muslims. Muhammad's word has been passed on: "The greatest of places is Jerusalem, and the greatest of rocks is the rock at Jerusalem." In A.D. 691 Calif Abd el-Malek erected the Dome of the Rock over the holy rock which was a part of the ancient Jewish temple. With its walls of glazed tile and its golden dome, it looks like the expensive setting for a jewel. According to Muslim tradition, it marks the place from which Muhammad was taken up into heaven.

The ownership of this place, along with that of the nearby Mosque of Aksa, is of the greatest importance for Islamic believers. To this day many Muslim pilgrims travel to these holy places. Thus the "Holy City" of Jerusalem has a firm place in Islamic piety.

Christians and Jerusalem

In Christianity there is a tradition reaching back to the New Testament which understands Jerusalem as a heavenly entity. According to Revelation 21, this new Jerusalem is the city where God lives and where, along with Jesus, God is worshiped by all nations. The wish expressed in the hymns, "Jerusalem, Whose Towers Touch the Skies, I Yearn to Come to You!" or "Jerusalem, My Happy Home, When Shall I Come to Thee?" is directed toward Jerusalem as a symbol of the future glorious life, in which there will be no more sorrow and no more death. This notion cannot be understood without the prototype of the earthly Jerusalem and its meaning for biblical faith. So Christians cannot look upon the problems arising from the opposing claims to Jerusalem and the land of the Bible as disinterested observers. As those who are the least directly involved, they have the special obligation to try to find ways to resolve the existing conflict.

In view of the deep roots of the various religious, historical, national, and political claims, it is apparent that there will be no simple solutions. Ways must be sought which deal fairly with the complicated entanglements and the apparently mutually exclusive claims, and which will lead to the forming of a community that can build bridges over the existing conflicts.

At present, peace does not exist in the Middle East. In the past, as well, conflict has repeatedly erupted. But it should not be forgotten that there have also been long periods of peace in this area. Conflict is by no means an inevitable characteristic of the Middle East.

The holy places in Jerusalem are under the administration of separate committees of Jews, Christians, and Muslims. Free access for believers of all faiths has been a reality since 1967.

The task for Jews, Christians, and Muslims today is to bring about peace in the land of the Bible, so that later generations can live, work, and pray in Jerusalem and in the entire land, with mutual respect for one another and without fear and hatred.

7

Religious Movements

According to the *American Jewish Yearbook, 1986,* there are some 13 million Jews in the world. Those countries with the largest Jewish populations are as follows:

United States	5.7 million
Israel	3.5 million
Soviet Union	1.6 million
France	530,000
Great Britain	330,000
Canada	310,000
Argentina	228,000
South Africa	118,000
Brazil	100,000

These statistics reflect the extermination of two-thirds of European Judaism during the Nazi period and the gathering of Jews in the State of Israel, as well as migration patterns from much earlier times.

Judaism has never been a unified entity, not even in matters of religion. The conflicts between Pharisees and Sadducees at the time of Jesus are well-known. In view of the great variety of conditions under which the Jews lived, it is not surprising that various movements in Judaism also emerged in later periods. What are the currents and movements within contemporary Judaism? How did these movements arise? What are the differences between Orthodox, Conservative, and Reform Jews? How do these religious movements within Judaism compare to the division of Christianity into denominations? These questions will be considered in this chapter.

Movements in Contemporary Judaism

As early as the Middle Ages, when Europe became the spiritual and cultural center of Jewish life, there developed alongside the "oriental" Judaism of Asia and southern Arabia two expressions of Jewish-religious life which are still operative: *Sephardic* Judaism in Spain and *Ashkenazic* Judaism in France and Germany.

Due primarily to persecution and oppression, but also to trade relationships and emigration, Sephardic Judaism spread and left its impression throughout the entire Mediterranean area and as far as the Near East. It also branched out to Holland, England, and northwestern Germany, as well as to America and other parts of the world.

Ashkenazic Judaism spread through Eastern Europe (especially Poland and Russia) and from there to Western Europe, America, Israel, and other areas of the world. The two groups differ in their pronunciation of Hebrew in the worship service, their different ways of worshiping (Sephardic and Ashkenazic rites) and their different folk customs and colloquial languages (Ashkenazic Jews speak Yiddish, a kind of German dialect). When Sephardic and Ashkenazic Jews live in the same area, they ordinarily assemble in their own synagogues in order to preserve their distinctiveness.

Within both of these traditions, which have existed for a very long time, there have always been tendencies toward a Jewish mysticism, such as the esoteric mysticism called "Kabbalah" or in the ecstatic piety of

Hasidism. Judaism today, however, is much more strongly marked by the movements which have developed only recently—Orthodox, Conservative, and Reform—than by the distinctions of the past.

How These Movements Developed

Until recently, the unifying bond for all Jews has been not only their common religious tradition (expressed in a variety of ways) but also their common fate, characterized above all by opposition from the Christian and Muslim world surrounding them. But in modern times the unity of the Jewish people has been threatened from both inside and out, as a result of the opening up of the ghettos, the gaining of equal rights with other citizens in the late 18th and early 19th centuries, and the idea of the equality of all human beings that was given expression during the Enlightenment. The process of assimilation into the surrounding culture, set in motion by these factors, has deeply affected modern Judaism. Just as confessional Christianity was diminished by this onslaught, so Jews who held to their traditional beliefs became a minority within Judaism, seeing themselves as having been put on the defensive.

The distinction between "Orthodox" and "liberal" in contemporary Judaism should be viewed against this background. The affirmation or denial of Judaism as a religion is not at issue. Rather, there are the Orthodox on the one side, who orient their lives according to religious tradition and who want to live in a manner which is in accord with the prescriptions of the Torah (the first five books of the Bible) and the Talmud (a collection of postbiblical writings). On the other side are the Reform Jews, who have changed, reformed,

73

and liberalized the traditions to fit the changed situation of the modern world. In between is the middle group, the Conservatives. Beyond these, there are great numbers within the Jewish people who are estranged from the faith of their ancestors and from the religious obligations of their community. There are many nonbelieving Jews who read the Bible only as a book containing their national history. There are even atheistic Jews who nevertheless feel themselves bound to the common fate of the Jewish people.

Zionism has awakened Jewish self-consciousness, in reaction to assimilation and anti-Semitism, and this movement in which Jews have worked together has contributed to a revival of the unity of the Jewish people. Since the era of the Holocaust, with its attempt to exterminate everything Jewish, and the establishment of the State of Israel, the Zionist idea has become more and more attractive, even among the various religious movements which at first adopted a cautious or a negative attitude toward it.

Orthodox, Conservative, and Reform Judaism

The outlook of *Orthodox* Judaism—which prefers to call itself "Torah-true"—can perhaps best be characterized by the beginning sentence of the *Teachings of the Sages* (the *Pirkei Avot* from the Talmud): "Moses received Torah from God at Sinai. He transmitted it to Joshua, Joshua to the elders, the elders to the prophets, the prophets to the members of the great assembly" (*Siddur Sim Shalom: A Prayerbook for Shabbat, Festivals, and Weekdays,* p. 603). Linked up with this chain of tradition, the Torah-true Orthodox are to this day authorized to preach the Sinai revelation to the people. The historical changes that have taken place in the world have had little effect on this tradition.

Orthodox Jews see their people in the special position of being witnesses before the world: they are obligated to obey all of God's commandments. The Sabbath, for example, must be strictly observed. Also, they are not to partake of pork or blood, and meat and milk cannot be consumed at the same meal; in other words, their eating and drinking is to be *kosher* or correct. They can often be identified by their distinctive clothing and hairstyle.

In the State of Israel, where Orthodox Judaism is represented by both a Sephardic and an Ashkenazic Chief Rabbi, these Torah-true Jews have had great public influence. The shutting down of public transportation on the Sabbath, dietary regulations for the military, and the monopoly which Orthodox rabbis have in connection with marriages and divorces are all due to the persistence of Orthodox representatives in the government.

Liberal or *Reform* Judaism believes in a progressive revelation and takes into account changes brought about by historical developments. The directives from God have been further developed outside the Torah tradition. The stress is on "ethical monotheism" as found in the Torah and in the prophetic books, and scholars freely take part in modern biblical research. Worship in Reform synagogues is characterized by the use of musical instruments, prayer mostly in the colloquial language, and preaching as a regular part of the service. The dietary laws are not usually observed. Hope for a personal Messiah "from the house of David" is replaced by the hope for a messianic time for humankind. Israel is to be a "light to the nations" on the way to brotherhood and peace. The hope for resurrection is more in terms of a spiritual than a bodily eternal life. Reform Judaism, which first arose in Germany, now has its center in the United States. In Israel it is represented by only a few small congregations.

Conservative Judaism is the name for a middle position, which also has most of its representatives in the United States. In regard to revelation, Conservative Jews think in a critical and enlightened manner, similar to Reform Jews. However, they emphasize Hebrew language and culture more strongly as a unifying bond for Jews. They would like to preserve as much religious tradition as possible and they see in religious law a guarantee for the solidarity of Judaism.

Jewish Movements and Christian Denominations

Christendom is made up of independent churches and confessional groups which have only recently, through the ecumenical movement and by other means, come to a stronger consciousness of what all Christians have in common. Judaism has never been so rigidly organized and so separated into groups. Jews do indeed gather in particular synagogue congregations according to their own backgrounds and religious orientations. But if only a few Jews from a variety of religious backgrounds live in one place, they will probably all be found in a single, unified congregation. Despite the variety and even the conflicts of their religious views, Jews are always aware that they have a common destiny and are a part of one people.

Moreover, in most larger communities where Jews are present, there are a number of Jewish agencies designed to deal with a variety of educational, social, and other needs. Jews of all persuasions—including nonreligious Jews—join in these common efforts.

PART THREE

JEWISH WORSHIP

8

Jewish Prayer

On what occasions do Jews pray? What are the special features of Jewish prayer? What are some characteristic Jewish prayers? How much do Jewish and Christian prayers have in common? These questions will be dealt with in this chapter.

When and Where Do Jews Pray?

For devout Jews, the whole of life is worship. The acknowledgment of God as Creator and Lord of the world and of one's own life, by means of praise and prayers of blessing, is central to the Jew's life of faith. So all the events during the course of a day or the course of a life are accompanied by prayers. Jews "awaken" the day with the morning prayer (*Shaharit*), the longest of the weekday prayers. In the morning prayer the individual commits himself or herself to the hand of God, remembers the Torah, which has been given to the people Israel as both gift and task, recites the confession of faith, and offers other prayers of praise, petition, and repentance.

The day concludes with the evening prayer, which takes up a number of elements from the morning prayer once again. In the evening prayer the day is summed up and forgiveness is asked for both the open and the hidden sins of the day. The prayer ends on a note of trust in God's peace and protection.

Prayers at mealtime also play an important role. They often have the characteristic form of the *Berakhah* or word of blessing (plural, *Berakhot*): "Praised

are you, Lord our God, King of the universe, who
. . . ." *Berakhot* can be said on a variety of occasions,
such as special events in nature or after receiving good
or bad news; human beings are called to praise God
for everything. There are special prayers for the important occasions along life's way—circumcision,
marriage, and death. In addition, there are prayers for
celebrations in the home as well as for worship services
with the congregation. When possible, one prays with
others.

This brief survey makes clear some of the similarities between the practice of Jewish and Christian
prayer. But what are some of the differences?

Special Characteristics of Jewish Prayer

After the destruction of the Jerusalem temple in A.D.
70, prayer gained new meaning for Judaism. As the
"sacrifice of praise offered by the lips," it took the
place of temple sacrifices, which were no longer possible. Since that time, Jewish worship has been prayer-
centered worship, in the family as well as in the synagogue. Over the centuries, a series of formal prayers,
composed in Hebrew, has been added to the prayers
of the Psalms. They have been collected, along with
all other texts needed for worship in both home and
synagogue, in the Jewish Prayerbook (*Siddur*); many
editions print a translation in the local language alongside the Hebrew.

In Orthodox services, only the men (13 years and
older) have liturgical roles in congregational worship.
In Reform and a growing number of Conservative congregations, women are also counted in the quorum
(*minyan*) and also take liturgical roles in the service.

In the home, both men and women have roles in worship.

Jewish prayer is connected with certain ritual actions. Before prayer, the hands are washed (also the face, at the time of morning prayer), at which time an appropriate *Berakhah* is spoken. At morning prayer at home or in the synagogue one wears a prayer shawl (*tallit*), a large, four-cornered shawl with tassels (*tzitzit*) on the corners. The head is always covered during prayer as a sign of humility before God. Phylacteries (*tefillin*) are worn during the daily morning prayer on weekdays, but not on Sabbath or holidays; these are small cubes containing scripture passages which are placed on the forehead and the left arm by means of leather straps. The cubes contain pieces of parchment on which are printed Deuteronomy 6:4-9; 11; 13–21 and Exod. 13:1-16. In putting these on "as a sign upon your hand, and . . . as frontlets between your eyes" (Deut. 6:8), the covenant bond with God is renewed each day. The beginning of the section in Deuteronomy 6 is written down in the *mezuzah,* a small container containing a scroll, which is then placed "on the doorposts of your house and on your gates" (Deut. 6:9). During prayer the hands are not folded; some who are praying move the upper part of the body back and forth, and some cover themselves completely with their prayer shawls.

The practice of prayer is very much the same in the various movements in Judaism. However, Reform Judaism allows more room for prayer in the local language, for free prayer, and for women taking part in liturgy, and rejects a number of the traditional customs associated with prayer.

Typical Jewish Prayers

Only a small selection of Jewish prayers can be given here. The *Shema* is the central prayer in Judaism and is at the same time a confession of faith: "Hear, O Israel: the Lord is our God, the Lord is one" (Deut. 6:4). It is supposed to be spoken daily, in the morning and evening prayer, and also in the hour of death; its text is found in the *tefillin* and also in the *mezuzah*. It is a call to faith in the one God.

The main prayer in worship—often called simply "prayer" (*tefillah*)—is the *Amidah,* recited while standing (which is the meaning of the Hebrew word). It is also called the "Prayer of 18 Petitions" (*Shemonah Esreh*), even though only the middle 13 blessings of the *Amidah* are petitions. To be more accurate, it consists of 19 (not 18) blessings. Its content has many points of contact with the Lord's Prayer. (The prayer is printed on pp. 86-89.)

One of the most-used Jewish prayers is the *Kaddish,* which is often also prayed by mourners:

Hallowed and enhanced may He be throughout the world of His own creation. May He cause His sovereignty soon to be accepted, during our life and the life of all Israel. And let us say: Amen.

Amen. May He be praised throughout all time!

Glorified and celebrated, lauded and praised, acclaimed and honored, extolled and exalted may the Holy One be, beyond all song and psalm, beyond all tributes which mortals can utter. And let us say: Amen.

May the prayers and pleas of the whole House of Israel be accepted by our Father in Heaven. And let us say: Amen.*

---

*When the Kaddish is used by mourners, this petition is omitted.

Let there be abundant peace from Heaven, with life's goodness for us and for all the people Israel. And let us say: Amen.

He who brings peace to His universe will bring peace to us and to all the people Israel. And let us say: Amen.

(*Siddur Sim Shalom: A Prayerbook for Shabbat, Festivals, and Weekdays*, pp. xvi-xvii.)

The litany *Avinu Malkenu* (Our Father, our King) is used during the 10 "Days of Repentance" between Rosh Hashanah and Yom Kippur, as well as on Fast Days. Each petition begins with this expression. A few are given here:

Avinu malkenu, we have sinned against You.

Avinu malkenu, we have no King but You.

Avinu malkenu, annul the plots of our enemies.

Avinu malkenu, send complete healing to the sick.

Avinu malkenu, inscribe us in the Book of forgiveness.

Avinu malkenu, hasten our deliverance.

Avinu malkenu, act for those slain for Your holy name.

Avinu malkenu, act for Your sake if not for ours.

Avinu malkenu, answer us though we have no deeds to plead our cause; save us with mercy and lovingkindness.

(*Siddur Sim Shalom: A Prayerbook for Shabbat, Festivals, and Weekdays*, pp. 125-127.)

Jewish and Christian Prayer

Jews and Christians share a common inheritance in the biblical Psalms, the roots of both traditions of prayer. The prayers of Judaism are as greatly influenced by the Psalms as are the prayers found in the New Testament and in a major part of Christian prayer literature. The hymns found in Luke 1 and 2 could be in a

Jewish prayerbook. The relationship between the Lord's Prayer and the 18 Petitions has often been pointed out. In prayer, Jews and Christians confess the same God as Creator, Lord, Sustainer, and Perfecter of the world. Both can bring praise and thanksgiving, lament and confession of sin, petition and intercession before the Lord in the same or similar words. And Jews see the whole of life as prayer; the New Testament understands life in this same way.

But Jewish and Christian prayers are not identical. There are great differences, not only in the way in which prayers are prayed, but also in the rites which accompany them. There are also considerable differences in the concept of human beings and their salvation, differences which are related to the fact that Christians pray to God "through Jesus Christ, our Lord." At this point there are unresolved problems between Christians and Jews. Therefore, attempts to bring Christians and Jews closer together through prayer should be considered carefully. Such attempts should respect the religious convictions of the participants and should be in the context of broad common efforts which do not neglect the questions still separating Jews and Christians.

Excerpt: The Amidah

Praised are You, Lord our God and God of our ancestors, God of Abraham, of Isaac, and of Jacob, great, mighty, awesome, exalted God who bestows lovingkindness, Creator of all. You remember the pious deeds of our ancestors and will send a redeemer to their children's children because of Your loving nature. You are the King who helps and saves and shields. Praised are You, Lord, Shield of Abraham.

Your might, O Lord, is boundless. You give life to the dead; great is Your saving power. Your lovingkindness sustains the living. Your great mercies give life to the dead. You support the falling, heal the ailing, free the fettered. You keep Your faith with those who sleep in dust. Whose power can compare with Yours? You are the Master of life and death and deliverance. Faithful are You in giving life to the dead. Praised are You, Lord, Master of life and death.

Holy are You and holy is Your name. Holy are those who praise You daily. Praised are You, Lord holy God.

You graciously endow mortals with intelligence, teaching wisdom and understanding. Grant us knowledge, discernment, and wisdom. Praised are You, Lord who graciously grants intelligence.

Our Father, bring us back to Your Torah. Our King draw us near to Your service. Lead us back to You, truly repentant. Praised are You, Lord, who welcomes repentance.

Forgive us, our Father, for we have sinned; pardon us, our King, for we have transgressed, for You forgive and pardon. Praised are You, gracious and forgiving Lord.

Behold our affliction and deliver us. Redeem us soon because of Your mercy, for You are the mighty Redeemer. Praised are You, Lord, Redeemer of the people Israel.

Heal us, O Lord, and we shall be healed. Help us and save us, for You are our glory. Grant perfect healing for all our afflictions. For You are the faithful and merciful God of healing. Praised are You, Lord, Healer of His people Israel.

Lord our God, make this a blessed year. May its varied produce bring us happiness. Grant blessing to the earth. Satisfy us with its abundance, and bless our year as the best of years. Praised are You, Lord who blesses the years.

Sound the great shofar to herald our freedom, raise high the banner to gather all exiles. Gather the dispersed from the ends of the earth. Praised are You, Lord who gathers our dispersed.

Restore our judges as in days of old, restore our counselors as in former times. Remove from us sorrow and anguish. Reign alone over us with lovingkindness; with justice and mercy sustain our cause. Praised are You, Lord, King who loves justice.

Frustrate the hopes of all those who malign us; let all evil very soon disappear. Let all Your enemies soon be destroyed. May You quickly uproot and crush the arrogant; may You subdue and humble them in our time. Praised are You, Lord who humbles the arrogant.

Let Your tender mercies be stirred for the righteous, the pious, and the leaders of the House of Israel, devoted scholars and faithful proselytes. Be merciful to us of the House of Israel. Reward all who trust in You, cast our lot with those who are faithful to You. May we never come to despair, for our trust is in You. Praised are You, Lord who sustains the righteous.

Have mercy, Lord, and return to Jerusalem, Your city. May Your Presence dwell there as You have promised. Build it now, in our days and for all time. Reestablish there the majesty of David, Your servant. Praised are You, Lord who builds Jerusalem.

Bring to flower the shoot of Your servant David. Hasten the advent of Messianic redemption. Each and every day we hope for Your deliverance. Praised are You, Lord who assures our deliverance.

Lord, our God, hear our voice. Have compassion on us, pity us, accept our prayer with loving favor. You listen to entreaty and prayer. Do not turn us away unanswered, our King, for You mercifully hear Your people's supplication. Praised are You, Lord who hears prayer.

Accept the prayer of Your people as lovingly as it is offered. Restore worship to Your sanctuary. May the worship of Your people Israel always be acceptable to You. May we witness Your merciful return to Zion. Praised are You, Lord who restores His Presence to Zion.

We proclaim that You are the Lord our God and God of our ancestors throughout all time. You are the Rock of our lives, the Shield of our salvation in every generation. We thank You and praise You morning, noon, and night for Your miracles which daily attend us and for Your wondrous kindnesses. Our lives are in Your hand; our souls are in Your charge. You are good, with everlasting mercy; You are compassionate, with enduring lovingkindness. We have always placed our hope in You. For all these blessings we shall ever praise and exalt You. May every living creature thank You and praise You faithfully, our deliverance and our help. Praised are You, beneficent Lord to whom all praise is due.

Grant peace to the world, with happiness, and blessing, grace, love, and mercy for us and for all the people Israel. Bless us, our Father, one and all, with Your light; for by that light did You teach us Torah and life, love and tenderness, justice, mercy, and peace. May it please You to bless Your people Israel in every season and at all times with Your gift of peace. Praised are You, Lord who blesses His people Israel with peace.

(Siddur Sim Shalom: A Prayerbook for Shabbat, Festivals, and Weekdays, pp. 107-121.)

9

The Jewish Festival Year

Christians and Jews have the seven-day week in common. Jews observe the seventh day (the Sabbath) as holy (see Exod. 20:9-10), and Christians the first day (Sunday, in remembrance of the resurrection of Jesus; see Mark 16:1-2). In addition, both Jews and Christians have special festivals during the course of the year. The festivals of contemporary Judaism (like the Christian festivals) have developed from the festivals of Old Testament times. They reenact the mighty acts of God in the history of God's people.

Jewish chronology begins with the creation of the world, which tradition calculates as the year 3760 (or 3761) before Christian chronology began (A.D. 2000 would thus be 5760/61 according to Jewish calculation). The Jewish year begins in the fall, after the farmers have completed the harvest. Dates in the Jewish year do not correspond to the solar calendar year because the Jewish year is made up of lunar months of either 29 or 30 days and therefore totals only 354 days; it is adjusted to the solar year with the periodic insertion of a leap month of 30 extra days. Thus the dates of the festivals can vary over several weeks when compared with the solar calendar, similar to the situation with the date for the Christian Easter, which is also based on lunar calculations.

The three "pilgrimage festivals" had their beginnings in biblical times: Passover, Shavuot (the Feast of Weeks), and Sukkot (the Feast of Booths). The same is true for Rosh Hashanah (New Year's Day) and Yom

Kippur (the Day of Atonement; see Exod. 23:14-17; Leviticus 23; Deuteronomy 16).

Passover (Hebrew, Pesach)

Passover celebrates the exodus, God's miraculous deliverance of the people from Egypt (see Exodus 12 and 13). The celebration is a high point of Jewish life and begins with the full moon in the month of *Nissan* (March/April); associated with it is the "Feast of Unleavened Bread" (the Hebrew word for unleavened bread is *matzot*). Preparations for the celebration in the home include getting rid of everything containing leaven; during the festival week, observant Jews do not eat or drink anything which is leavened or fermented.

Before the destruction of the Jerusalem temple in A.D. 70, the Passover lambs were sacrificed and eaten there. Since the destruction, the Passover lamb has been symbolically represented by a roasted shankbone. The Passover meal is family celebration, home worship, and festival meal all in one (see pp. 102-105). At Passover, family members and friends or congregational groups gather together. The celebration follows a certain order (*seder*) and is thus called a "seder."

Everyone seated at the festively decorated table has a *haggadah* (story), a book containing texts arranged in an order for worship. Usually the father of the household presides. Together with all present, he chants the words of blessing over the four cups of wine, the unleavened bread, and the food which is part of the festival. After the youngest has asked, "Why is this night different from all other nights?" the father leads the psalm singing and recites the story of the exodus from Egypt. Singing folk songs is a part of the celebration.

The jumping-off point for the Passover celebration is the telling of the story of the exodus. The conversation around the table then turns to contemporary manifestations of enslavement and liberation, and may go on for hours. Worship services in the synagogue at Passover time are especially elaborate.

The Christian festival of Easter as the celebration of the resurrection of Jesus preserves the connection with Passover by its date, among other things; there are also connections between the Lord's Supper and the Passover meal; for example, in the use of unleavened bread for Communion.

Shavuot

Shavuot, which means "weeks," takes place seven weeks (hence its name) or 50 days (in Greek, *pentecoste,* from which we get Pentecost) after Passover. According to the agricultural year, it was the day for completing the barley harvest and for bringing the offering of the firstfruits. In the post-biblical era it became, above all, the festival for remembering God's revelation on Mount Sinai (Exodus 19–20).

Special services are conducted on the day of Shavuot which include a dramatized reading of the account of the giving of the Ten Commandments. On Shavuot eve, congregations have all-night study sessions, to reenact the scene at Mount Sinai when, according to tradition, no one slept, in anticipation of receiving the Torah. In many agricultural communities in Israel, the ancient agricultural aspect of the festival of firstfruits is observed with pageants of song and dance.

As the Christian festival of the outpouring of the Holy Spirit, Pentecost goes back to an event which happened at the festival of *Shavuot* (see Acts 2). As with Easter and Passover, the dates are also related: Pentecost is celebrated 50 days after Easter.

Sukkot

This festival takes its name from the booths or huts (*sukkot*) in which observant Jews spend many hours during the festival week, studying Torah and also eating meals (see "Celebrations in the Home," pp. 105-106). It begins with the full moon of the fall month *Tishri* (September/October). Associated with *Sukkot* are thanksgiving for the harvest and prayer for rain. Above all, this festival recalls the time of the wandering in the wilderness, when the Israelites lived in temporary shelters.

Those worshiping in the synagogue carry bouquets made up of four different plants (branches from a date palm, myrtles, willows, and citron). Since the Middle Ages, the last day of the festival has been *Simhat Torah* (Joy in the Torah). On this day the annual reading of the first five books of the Old Testament is completed and the cycle begins anew with Genesis 1. The customs of the festival present the Torah as the source of joy. In the worship service, all the Torah scrolls are carried around the lectern seven times in a festive, dancing procession in which the children, especially, are involved. In Israel the exuberant dancing and singing with the Torah scrolls spills out into the streets with great joy and abandon.

The Christian church year has nothing which corresponds to *Sukkot;* the American Thanksgiving Day has a similar theme.

The blowing of the *shofar* at the beginning of the Passover Pilgrimage to Mount Zion, Jerusalem.

Rosh Hashanah (New Year's Day)

Tishri (September/October) is the month of the High Holy Days. It begins with the festival of the new year, which is celebrated for two days. Characteristic of this festival are the sounds of the *shofar* (ram's horn), at times like a trumpet call, at times long and drawn out, recalling the ram which was offered by Abraham in place of Isaac (Genesis 22). The festival serves as a day of examination for all people, the examiner being the righteous and merciful Creator.

Yom Kippur (Day of Atonement)

Yom Kippur falls on the 10th of *Tishri* (Leviticus 16). For Jews, this is the most important and most personal holy day. Hardly anyone can evade its demands entirely. It is celebrated with the greatest solemnity as a day of complete fasting, with no food or water. For the all-day worship service, many worshipers wear the white garments in which they will one day be buried.

In biblical times, Yom Kippur was the only day of the year in which the high priest entered the holiest place in the temple, to sprinkle it with the blood from sacrificial animals. In another ceremony, the sins of the people were symbolically placed on a goat, which was then sent into the wilderness as the "scapegoat" (Lev. 16:20-22).

None of this has been carried out since the destruction of the temple. But the meaning of Yom Kippur as the time for settlement of sins remains. Congregational confession of sins before God is a large part of the worship service. (The private making of amends and requests for forgiveness from other persons takes place before the service.) The *Kol Nidre* (all vows) is a characteristic Yom Kippur song. It is a prayer for the release of the obligation from unfulfilled religious vows, well-known beyond the boundaries of Judaism because of its haunting melody.

Christianity has nothing which corresponds directly to Yom Kippur. Christians in some countries observe special days of repentance and prayer. Roman Catholic Christians preserve the practice of individual confession. In each of these cases, sins are confessed and forgiveness is declared.

Hanukkah (Feast of Dedication, Feast of Lights)

This eight-day festival begins on the evening of the 24th of *Kislev* (November/December) and recalls the rededication of the temple in the year 164 B.C., after the sanctuary had been saved from the dangers of desecration and from being taken over by pagans (see 1 Macc. 4:51-59; 2 Macc. 10:1-8). Each day one more candle is lit on an eight-branched candelabrum called a menorah. A ninth candle, called the *shamash* (servant), is used to light the others. Menorahs are placed in windows or doorways as a witness to Judaism.

Because Hanukkah frequently comes near Christmastime, in Christian surroundings it has taken over many features of this festival, such as sending greeting cards and giving presents. Beyond these superficial details, however, the two festivals have no connection with each other.

Purim

This is a joyful holiday commemorating the deliverance from the danger of persecution, taking place on the 14th day of the month *Adar* (outside Israel, Purim is also celebrated on the 15th). The biblical book of Esther tells about a persecution of the Jews which was to take place in ancient times, but which was averted by the courage of Esther. The villain, Haman, becomes a symbol of those who hate the Jews. The scroll of Esther is read during the worship service; each time Haman is mentioned, adults and children alike make noise with noisemakers of all sorts, including rattles especially designed for the occasion, called "groggers." In modern-day Israel, the festival of Purim is celebrated with great exuberance and has the marks of a carnival. Children often march in parades with colorful costumes.

Fast Days

Scattered throughout the year are a few days of general mourning and fasting which recall events connected with the first destruction of the Jerusalem temple. The most important of these days is the *Ninth of Ab* (July/August), the day on which the temple was destroyed in 587 B.C. and also in A.D. 70. This is a 24-hour fast day. In the worship service the biblical book of Lamentations is read, as well as laments coming from the persecutions of the Jews in the Middle Ages. Thus the *Ninth of Ab* is something of a national day of sorrow.

For Christians in some countries, the 11th Sunday after Pentecost—earlier often observed as a memorial day for the destruction of Jerusalem—has become a day for considering the relationship between the church and Judaism. Lutherans have a rubric for a "Day of Penitence" which "may coincide with a local remembrance of the Holocaust" (*Lutheran Book of Worship,* p. 39).

The Jewish Calendar, with Major Festivals
(Biblical origins indicated where applicable)

Tishri (September/October) 30 Days
  1. Rosh Hashanah I (Lev. 23:23-25)
  2. Rosh Hashanah II
  10. Yom Kippur (Lev. 23:26-32)
  15. Sukkot I (Lev. 23:33-36; Deut. 16:13-17)
  16. Sukkot II
  22. Sukkot VIII
  23. Simhat Torah

Heshvan (October/November) 29 Days

Kislev (November/December) 30 Days
25. Hanukkah I (Maccabees)

Tevet (December/January) 29 Days
3. Hanukkah VIII

Shevat (January/February) 30 Days

Adar (February/March) 29 Days
14. Purim (Book of Esther)

Nisan (March/April) 30 Days
15. Pesach I (Exodus 12; Lev. 23:4-8; Deut. 16:1-8)
16. Pesach II
21. Pesach VII
22. Pesach VIII
27. Yom ha-Shoa (Day of Holocaust)

Iyyar (April/May) 29 Days
5. Yom ha-Atzmaut (Day of Independence)

Sivan (May/June) 30 Days
6. Shavuot I (Exod. 19-20; Lev. 23:15-21; Deut. 16:9-12)
7. Shavuot II

Tammuz (June/July) 29 Days

Ab (July/August) 30 Days

9. Tishah be-Ab (Ninth of Ab, Fast Day)

Elul (August/September) 29 Days

Excerpt from a Yom Kippur Prayer

Man's origin is dust and his end is dust. He spends his life earning bread. He is like a clay vessel, easily broken, like withering grass, a fading flower, a passing shadow, a fugitive cloud, a fleeting breeze, scattering dust, a vanishing dream.

(*Mahzor for Rosh Hashanah and Yom Kippur,* p. 539.)

Excerpt from the Concluding Prayer (Ne'eelah) at Yom Kippur

You extend a welcome to transgressors, ready to embrace all those who turn in repentance. You have taught us to confess all our sins to You, that we may cease doing violence to our lives. Accept us in wholehearted repentance, as You have promised.

Open for us the gates, even as they are closing.
The day is waning, the sun is low
The hour is late, a year has slipped away.
Let us enter the gates at last.
Lord, have compassion. Pardon, forgive, take pity.
Grant us atonement. Help us to conquer our iniquity and sin.

(*Mahzor for Rosh Hashanah and Yom Kippur,* pp. 715, 731.)

10

Celebrations in the Home

Celebrations in the home have great meaning in the religious life of Jewish people. Worship in the synagogue and religious observances in the home are connected with one another and are mutually supportive. They are two sides of one reality, life before God. That is why a Jewish family can practice a fully authentic worship life in home celebrations, even if it is not possible for them to worship in a synagogue. This has been characteristic of Judaism since Old Testament times.

Christians often know only the rules for these practices, which they perceive as legalistic constraints. But the real purpose of these rules is to create space for the life of worship. How do Jews understand and experience the celebrations in the home? Three examples will illustrate.

The Celebration of the Sabbath

In the rhythm of their lives, devout Jews are to emulate the action of God: the Sabbath "is a sign for ever between me and the people of Israel that in six days the Lord made heaven and earth, and on the seventh day he rested, and was refreshed" (Exod. 31:17; see Gen. 2:2-3; Exod. 20:8-11). The Sabbath took its form at an early time, not only with regard to the observance of certain commandments and rest from work, but also in the shaping of its celebration in the home.

In the life of a devout Jew, the whole week is directed toward the Sabbath. Friday already has a festive character, because the Sabbath begins on that evening. One buys good food, bakes special bread called *hallah* in the form of a braid, decorates the house, bathes, and dresses in a festive manner. The Sabbath is to be received like a queen or a bride.

The woman of the house, who usually does not have an independent part in Jewish worship, has an almost priestly role in the family Sabbath celebration. She greets the entering Sabbath by lighting the two Sabbath candles and saying a blessing over them.

If it is possible to take part in a Friday evening synagogue service, one hurries home afterward in order to continue the celebration there. Usually the father is in charge: he greets the Sabbath by saying, *"Gut Shabbos"* or *"Shabbat Shalom,"* recites the praise of the "woman of valor" (Prov. 31:10-31), and chants the *Kiddush*, the blessing of the day, with even more ceremony than is included in the synagogue service. Then he raises the cup filled to the rim with wine, drinks from it, and passes it around, even to the youngest child.

After the ceremonial hand washing and the table prayer ("Praised are You, Lord our God, King of the universe, who brings forth bread from the earth"), the head of the household begins the meal by cutting and passing out a piece of Sabbath bread for each person present. The Sabbath meal is to be as beautiful and festive as possible, because on the Sabbath, "every Jew is a king in his own house." Sabbath songs are sung, concluding with Psalm 126.

The Sabbath continues on Saturday, with worship in the synagogue, a good dinner at noon, and much rest. The evening meal is as late as possible, in order to extend the peace and joy of the Sabbath. The father bids the Sabbath farewell with the *Havdalah* (separation) ceremony: once again a glass of wine (or juice or milk) is passed around, then an ornamental box of sweet-smelling spices. The *Havdalah* candle allows the light of the Sabbath to shine into the coming week.

The Celebration of Passover

The Passover festival looks back to Israel's beginnings, when God cared for them and delivered them from Egypt. This festival—called *Pesach* in Hebrew—goes on for eight days and is celebrated chiefly in the home. Intensive preparations precede it. Since it is the "Festival of Unleavened Bread," that is, of *matzot,* before the festival the Jewish home is thoroughly searched for anything leavened. All kitchen utensils, including dishes, pots, and cutlery, must be cleansed of any trace of leaven, or made *kosher* ("correct"; see 1 Cor. 5:7, "Cleanse out the old leaven . . ."). The *matzot,* baked out of wheat flour without leaven or yeast, can be purchased at bakeries which specialize in making them or sometimes in supermarkets. They are to be a reminder that on the day before the exodus from Egypt there was no time to let the bread rise.

On the first evening of Passover, the celebration in the synagogue is not much different from other evening services. The real festival begins at home with the *seder* to which friends, poor people, and even non-Jews are gladly invited.

The table is set in a festive manner. There is a cup of wine for each person present, and in the middle of the table is the large seder plate. On it are three *matzot;* a vegetable (such as horseradish), as a reminder of the

A table prepared for the seder meal.

bitter suffering in Egypt; a pastelike dish made of apples or figs, nuts, and wine and given the color of clay by the addition of cinnamon (a reminder that in Egypt the Israelites had to make bricks out of clay); a hard-boiled egg, a symbol of the temple sacrifices; and a roasted shankbone from a lamb (or a roasted chicken) as a reminder of the Passover lamb slaughtered at the time of the exodus in Egypt and later in the temple.

The Passover festival is not intended to be just a reminder of the exodus from Egypt. "All persons, of both sexes and of every age, are to regard themselves as if they personally had been delivered from Egypt." Everything is aimed at a reenactment of what took place at that time: "The Lord has delivered us from Egypt!"

Usually the woman of the house looks after the decorations and the physical well-being of all present, and the man presides at the celebration. He opens it with prayer. The first cup of wine is drunk, a *matzah* is broken in two, and the halves are distributed. Then the seder plate is lifted up: "This is the bread of poverty which our fathers ate in Egypt. Whoever is hungry, come and eat! Whoever is distressed, come and celebrate Passover with us! This year we are here—next year in the land of Israel! This year we celebrate as slaves—next year as free!" In response to the four prescribed questions asked by the youngest person at the table, all recite the story of the exodus from Egypt, with the help of the *Haggadah,* which is both a story book and an order for worship. The various items on the seder plate are explained, psalms are sung, and then the ritual foods are eaten and the second cup of wine is drunk.

After this comes the actual evening meal, introduced with the breaking of bread and with prayer. All eat their fill. After the third cup of wine comes the "Great *Hallel*" (Psalms 113–118; 136), then more songs which express the wish for a speedy redemption through the coming of the Messiah. This wish climaxes in the cry, "Next year in Jerusalem!" (in modern-day Israel, often in "rebuilt Jerusalem!"). The fourth cup of wine is drunk and the celebration comes to a close with folk songs which tell of the mighty acts of God and the troubles and hope of Israel. A fifth cup of wine, set out for the prophet Elijah, remains full.

The Passover festival is no doubt the most intimate of Judaism's festivals. It has its established place in Jewish families throughout the entire world.

The Celebration of Sukkot

The life of the Jewish family is involved in the celebration of *sukkot* even more completely than in the weekly celebration of Sabbath or the yearly festival of Passover. In remembrance of the wandering in the wilderness, when the Israelites had to live in temporary huts, Jewish families spend as much time as possible during the festival week in *sukkot*, or specially constructed huts. They will eat meals in the *sukkah* and some will sleep there. One is supposed to be able to see the stars through the roof. These *sukkot* are often artistically decorated. Once again, the purpose of this festival is not just to serve as a reminder, but to "contemporize" the experiences of the generation that lived in the wilderness. When the Jewish family leaves the security of its house and moves into the *sukkah,* they experience anew their dependence on God and know themselves to be hidden in God's unchanging faith-fulness.

The Importance of Celebrations in the Home

These are some examples of the ways in which worship takes place in the home life of the Jewish people. We have presented an ideal picture; the realities may fall short of the ideal to greater or lesser degrees. However, it cannot be denied that these observances in Jewish homes make a decisive contribution to the preservation of Judaism. They make it possible for Jews to live and to experience their Judaism in the sphere of home and family.

According to a widespread Christian notion, the most essential part of a festival takes place as the congregation worships together in the church. That which takes place in the home is often a purely family affair without any religious connections. No such separation is found in Judaism. In following the Jewish example, Christians could rediscover the joy of a celebration in which the family worships together in the home.

11

Rites of Passage

For the devout Jew, all of life is worship. A Jew testifies to this with daily prayers, Sabbath worship, and the celebration of the yearly festivals. The decisive turning points along life's way, sometimes called "rites of passage," are also marked by religious observances.

What are these Jewish observances like? Where are the points of contact with Christian practices?

Circumcision (B'rit Milah)

Circumcision was practiced by a number of peoples in the ancient Near East. Today it is also practiced in Islam. Certain African, Asian, Australian, and oceanic tribes also circumcise, in some cases at the time of puberty. Circumcision has also been used as a routine medical procedure.

For the Israelites, ever since earliest times, circumcision has been the sign of the Abrahamic covenant between God and God's people (see Gen. 17:9-14; Lev. 12:3). A Jewish boy is ordinarily circumcised on the eighth day after his birth.

The circumcision takes place as follows: The one who does the circumcising (the *mohel*) removes the foreskin (*milah*) of the penis with a knife—which in ancient times was usually made of stone. Before the circumcision, which can take place in the synagogue, hospital, or home, the child is laid on a special chair, the "Chair of Elijah." Elijah is the prophet Jews consider to be God's eternal messenger to God's people.

During the circumcision, the godfather (the *sandek*) holds the child on his lap. The father gives thanks to God for the good fortune that the child has been incorporated into the covenant with Abraham, and then the *mohel* strikes up a song of praise for the commandment of circumcision. Giving the child a name is also a part of the rite of circumcision. A festive meal follows, at which time the guests give presents.

There is no such ceremony for girls; the name-giving usually takes place in the synagogue on the first Sabbath after the baby girl's birth.

If the circumcised boy is the firstborn, then the "redemption" must take place 30 days after the birth (cf. Exod. 13:11-15), because the firstfruits of the harvest as well as the firstborn among animals and human beings belong to God. The amount of five "shekels" is presented to a member of a priestly family (a *cohen*) as the payment for redeeming the child. The firstborn of priestly families do not need to be redeemed.

The New Testament mentions the circumcision of Jesus and his presentation in the temple (Luke 2:21-24). The Jewish-Christian church retained the practice of circumcision, but for Gentile Christians the obligation of circumcision was canceled (see Acts 15). In Judaism, new converts are ritually immersed or "baptized" in a bath called a *mikvah*. The first-century Jewish practice of baptism was the forerunner of Christian Baptism, in which all believers are incorporated into God's covenant in Jesus Christ.

Bar Mitzvah and Bat Mitzvah

The content of the religious upbringing of a Jewish child is the step-by-step introduction into life under the instruction of the Torah. This instruction is, first of all, the task of the parents. Beginning with the learning of prayers, further instruction in the directives of the Torah is supposed to continue at each age level. The congregation is responsible for providing a program of religious education.

At age 13 a Jewish boy reaches the age of religious responsibility, that is, he is now obligated to keep all the commandments of the Torah and becomes a "Son of the Commandment" (*Bar Mitzvah*). From this time on he is to put on the phylacteries (*tefillin*) for weekday morning prayer and he may be counted in the quorum of 10 (*minyan*) needed for public worship. At his Bar Mitzvah, on the Sabbath after his 13th birthday, a boy is invited to read from the Torah in the synagogue worship service for the first time in his life, and usually also delivers a speech. A festive meal, often an elaborate celebration, follows.

Girls become religiously responsible at the age of 12; that is, they are then obligated to live according to the rules of the Torah. In most Reform and Conservative congregations there is a *Bat Mitzvah* (Daughter of the Commandment) celebration which is similar to the Bar Mitzvah. Some Orthodox congregations have a modified Bat Mitzvah ceremony.

The *Bar Mitzvah* celebration arose in the Middle Ages, but it goes back to more ancient customs (see the story of the 12-year-old Jesus in the temple, Luke 2:41-52). The Christian practice of confirmation is based on similar ideas.

Marriage

For Jews, the marriage ceremony is one of the most important celebrations in life. Marriage and family are held in the highest regard. All Jews, including rabbis,

109

are encouraged to marry. A wedding is an event involving not just the two partners, but the entire congregation. When two people are married, the congregation sees the hope for the continuation of the people of Israel confirmed.

In earlier times, an engagement preceded the wedding. During the time of engagement, the bride was legally counted as a wife and unfaithfulness could be strictly punished (see Matt. 1:18-25; Luke 2:5). Today, however, engagement and marriage are part of one ceremony. The marriage ceremony takes place under a canopy (*huppah*) which is carried on four poles. This canopy symbolizes the couple's home, which they are to regard as a holy place.

After the blessing over the wine and over the betrothal of the couple, the bridegroom and bride drink from the wine. Then the marriage is completed with the bridegroom's declaration (in the presence of at least two witnesses): "By this ring you are consecrated to me as my wife in accordance with the Law of Moses and the people Israel." Then he places the ring on the forefinger of the bride's right hand. The marriage contract (*ketubah*) which has been prepared and signed earlier is read. In this contract the bridegroom promises that he will honor his wife, work for her, care for her, and provide all that is necessary for her livelihood. An address by the rabbi may follow. Then the "Seven Marriage Benedictions" are pronounced.

The ceremony ends with the breaking of a glass in remembrance of the destruction of the temple, and the best wishes of all present are offered. The concluding celebration begins with a festive meal and, among the more traditional, continues through seven evenings.

There is a rich tradition of wedding dances and sumptuous feasting.

As in Christian weddings, Judaism uses double marriage vows. For a divorce, which is allowed under certain prescribed conditions, a written document (called a *get*) is required, just as for a wedding (see Deut. 24:1-4).

Mourning Customs

Jews take for granted that death goes with life, just as night goes with day. A Jew is supposed to be prepared for death every day. When a person knows that death is near, he or she prepares for dying. One's affairs are brought in order, one prays the confession of sins (which is a part of the liturgy of *Yom Kippur*) in the first-person singular, and one blesses one's children. When death comes, those present and the one dying confess their faith in the oneness of God. The last word of the *shema Israel*, ". . . the Lord is one [*achad*]," should be spoken with one's last breath (Deut. 6:4).

The body should at first remain untouched. Those who are present demonstrate their sorrow by tearing a piece of clothing. Along with this act they speak the words which will be spoken again when the report of death goes out, "Praised be the One who judges in truth!" as well as other prayers. Then the body is laid on the earth and a candle is lit.

After the body has been washed, it is clothed in a simple, white, linen burial garment. The men and women of the "Holy Fellowship" (*Hevrah Kadishah*), a group found in most congregations, help with all arrangements in connection with death and burial. Immediate relatives of the deceased person are released from all religious obligations until after the burial.

The burial takes place one or two days after death. In Judaism, there is no embalming, no open casket, and no wake. Nor is the body's appearance altered by cosmetics. Judaism has also always rejected cremation. Burial is not allowed on the Sabbath or on a Jewish holiday. Each of those present throws three shovelfuls of dirt on the coffin. The most important prayer is the *kaddish*, which praises the name of God. The mourners walk away from the grave through the lane formed by the funeral guests, who speak words of comfort to them. The burial garment and a simple coffin and tombstone testify that in death all are equal.

The time of mourning begins with seven days (*shivah*) during which time the mourners sit on the ground or on low stools, as did those who mourned the destroyed sanctuary in Jerusalem. They refrain from work and read from the book of Job or from Jeremiah. Only the Sabbath interrupts this week of mourning. The second phase of mourning follows, lasting until the 30th day (*sheloshim*) after the death.

At every worship service for the next 11 months after the death of a parent, the *kaddish* for the departed is prayed. A candle is lit on the anniversary of the death. The tombstone is put in place anytime after *sheloshim*, usually on the first anniversary (*Yahrzeit*) of the death. At every following *Yahrzeit*, the one who died is once again remembered. Acts of kindness to those who are suffering are especially important during the period of mourning.

Jewish and Christian Celebrations

As is the case with Christians, the forms for the observance of the rites of passage will differ within Judaism, according to the country and the movement (such as Reform, Conservative, or Orthodox). In surveying the basic elements of Jewish celebrations, their similarities to the corresponding Christian observances are striking. Both religions have developed out of the same biblical and early rabbinic background.

Excerpt from the Wedding Service

After the blessing of the marriage over a glass of wine, the bridegroom places the ring on the forefinger of the bride's right hand and says:

By this ring you are consecrated to me as my wife in accordance with the Law of Moses and the people of Israel.

The nuptial agreement (*Ketubah*) is read and the seven marriage benedictions are recited or chanted:

We praise You, Lord our God, King of the universe who creates the fruit of the vine.

We praise You, Lord our God, King of the universe who created all for His glory.

We praise You, Lord our God, King of the universe, Creator of mortals.

We praise You, Lord our God, King of the universe who created male and female in His image, that together they might perpetuate life. We praise You, Lord, Creator of mortals.

May Zion rejoice as her children return to her in joy. We praise You, Lord who causes Zion to rejoice in her children.

Grant perfect joy to these loving companions, as You did for the first creatures in the Garden of Eden. We praise You, Lord who creates the joy of bride and groom.

We praise You, Lord our God, King of the universe who created joy and gladness, bride and groom, pleasure, song, delight, and happiness, love and harmony, peace and companionship. Lord our God, may there always be heard in the cities of Judah and in the streets of Jerusalem voices of joy and gladness, voices of bride and groom, the jubilant voices of those joined in marriage under the bridal canopy, the voices of young people feasting and singing. We praise You, Lord who causes the groom and the bride to rejoice together.

(*Siddur Sim Shalom: A Prayerbook for Shabbat, Festivals and Weekdays*, p. 773).

12

Worship in the Synagogue

Many Christians would like to find out more about Jewish worship and would like to visit a worship service in a synagogue. Such a visit is easily arranged. Christian and Jewish worship services have a common foundation in the biblical tradition. Both have scripture reading, prayer, and song as essential elements, and both usually follow a particular order of worship (a liturgy) and involve the participation of the entire congregation.

There are, however, many differences between Jews and Christians in the manner in which the presence of God in the worship service is represented and experienced. Christian worship is related to Jesus Christ, as is especially expressed in the sacraments of Baptism and the Lord's Supper. Jewish worship is especially oriented toward the Torah, and has incorporated elements from the offering of sacrifices in the temple, in the form of prayers (offerings of praise).

As in Christian congregations, the order of worship is not exactly the same in each Jewish congregation. Here the differences between Orthodox, Conservative, and Reform synagogues can clearly be seen. In America, while all three forms of Judaism are present, Conservative and Reform types of worship are especially prevalent. Despite the differences, there is a good deal of uniformity in the structure of the worship service.

What Seems Unusual about Jewish Worship?

Synagogues are as varied in their arrangement as are Christian churches; but the ark (*aron hakodesh*) or shrine where the Torah scrolls are kept is always visible in the front of the worship area. Between it and the congregation is the lectern (for the cantor) and the pulpit. The large reading desk for reading the Torah (*alemmor*) is often in the center of the room. There is no altar, and usually there is no organ.

Jewish worship is worship by the lay people, and requires their active participation. In Orthodox synagogues, the main worship service can begin only when 10 men (a *minyan*) age 13 or over have assembled. In Conservative and Reform congregations, women may be counted in the *minyan*. In Conservative and Reform synagogues, the men and women sit together; in Orthodox congregations, the women are seated separately. The worship service does not require the presence of a member of a priestly or levitical family (a Cohen or a Levi) or a rabbi (strictly speaking, one who is learned in Scripture, who advises the congregation and makes decisions in religious matters). In principle, the office of prayer leader, or cantor (*chazan*) can be held by anyone, but most American synagogues have a paid cantor on their staff. The men of the congregation (in Reform and Conservative synagogues, also the women) take their turns at reading the Torah.

In Jewish worship, piety expresses itself in forms not familiar to Christians: Men cover their heads with hats or a small cap called a *kipah* (or, from the Yiddish, a *yarmulke*). During daytime worship, including the morning of the Sabbath, the men wear four-cornered prayer shawls called *tallits*. Many worshipers move rhythmically back and forth during prayer. A visitor may be struck by seeing individuals come to the service late, leave early, or walk out and come back; in "the Father's house" a person ought to feel completely at home!

Orthodox services are almost entirely in Hebrew. In Conservative worship, and increasingly in Reform services, scripture readings and prayers are in Hebrew, while the sermon and other parts of the service are in the local language. The prayer for the country where the worshipers are living is also in the local language. In Orthodox and some Conservative synagogues, Friday evening services begin at sunset. In Reform and most Conservative congregations, they begin later Friday evening, after the evening meal. Friday evening services in Conservative and Reform synagogues are about one hour in length. The Sabbath morning services may last for two or three hours. Reform services are shorter than Orthodox or Conservative.

What Seems Familiar in Jewish Worship?

Some rabbis and cantors wear robes like those of Protestant pastors. This is not a Jewish custom, but goes back to a decree made by the Prussian King Friedrich Wilhelm III.

Even those who do not know Hebrew will quickly notice that the prayers conclude with the familiar *Amen*. The *Hallelujah* (Praise God!) and other exclamations in the prayers will also be familiar. The chanting of prayers and readings may remind the visitor of chanting in Christian worship. This practice goes back to worship in the temple. In addition to chanting, one also hears melodies which are similar to old folk tunes.

The Prayerbook (*siddur*) is the worship book, prayerbook, and songbook all in one, containing the same texts for use by the congregation, cantor, and rabbi. Most often it has texts in Hebrew and in English (or in the local language) side by side, so that those who do not know Hebrew can also participate.

What Happens at the Sabbath Morning Service?

The Sabbath begins on Friday evening (Gen. 1:5: "And there was evening and there was morning, one day") with an evening service in the synagogue and a celebration in the home. The main worship service is held on Saturday morning.

The Sabbath worship begins with some lengthy *prayers,* which are a part of the regular daily prayers. These are made up of psalms, meditations, and thanks to the Creator and Father, as well as instructional pieces about sacrifices in the ancient temple.

Following this is the *reading of Scripture.* This begins with the ceremonial opening of the ark containing the Torah, and the "raising" of the handwritten Torah scrolls, which are kept in a velvet or wood case and decorated with ornaments. The Torah is carried to the reading desk, taken out of its covering, and rolled out to the section of text appointed for that Sabbath (the *sidra* or pericope; see pp. 121-123).

After this, seven men are called to the Torah, one after the other, with any who are members of the Cohen or Levi families (understood to be descendants of the ancient priests and Levites) called first. In Reform and Conservative synagogues, women are also called to the Torah. At the beginning and the end of a subsection, they recite the Torah blessing. Reading according to the traditional chant melodies is done by the cantor. As the words are read, they are pointed out with a pointer called a *yad* (hand); out of reverence, the text of the scroll is not touched with the hand.

After the reading of the Torah, a text from the prophetic part of the Bible (*haftarah*) is chanted from a printed edition of the Hebrew Bible. The reading of

An Ashkenazic cantor in Jerusalem sings the prayers of Rosh Hashanah.

Scripture is concluded with the returning of the Torah scroll to the ark. In some non-Orthodox congregations the reading is shorter.

After this, especially in Conservative or Reform congregations, a *sermon* may follow. Sometimes there may be an afternoon study group.

The *concluding prayer* portion of the service includes prayers from the Psalms and also traditional prayers from the postbiblical era. Also included (as in the opening prayer portion of the service) is the *Shema* (Deut. 6:4), the "Jewish confession of faith." The priestly blessing, "The Lord bless you and keep you . . . " (Num. 6:24-26), familiar as a part of Christian worship, is also a part of this portion of the service, and is pronounced by the cantor; on holidays it is often given by descendants of priestly families in an especially ceremonial manner. The *kaddish*—a prayer which praises God in the hope of the coming of God's kingdom and which remembers the dead—frames the individual parts of the service. The worshipers stand for the *kaddish*, as well as for the raising and returning of the Torah and for the main prayer.

A Few Suggestions for Arranging a Synagogue Visit

Since service times are often tied to the rising and setting of the sun (which varies with the season of the year), it will be important to find out when the service begins. One can also find out which texts from the Torah and the prophets will be read that day and what places are available for guests. A visit with the rabbi or the cantor or with members of the congregation, either before or after the service, can usually be arranged.

Male visitors to the synagogue will be given a small cap or *kipah;* in many congregations women will cover their hair. Synagogues provide Bibles or prayerbooks for visitors so that they can follow the readings and the service. During the service, visitors should of course stand and sit when the congregation does.

The Jewish Lectionary (Weekly Bible Readings)

The first five biblical books (the Torah) are read during the course of the year in synagogue worship. To enable this, the Torah is divided into 54 sections, with one section assigned to each week. Because of the peculiarities of the Jewish calendar, the assignment of readings to a particular Sabbath day does not remain the same, but must be determined anew for each year. Occasionally several sections must be read on one Sabbath. Similar inconsistencies occur with lectionaries used for the Christian church year.

Each individual section of Torah (called a *sidrah*) has a name, which as a rule is taken from the opening words of the section. A reading from the prophets (called a *haftarah*) goes with each *sidrah:* readings from the "former prophets" (Joshua, Judges, 1-2 Samuel, 1-2 Kings) are also included. The series of readings is concluded and begins anew each year on *Simhat Torah,* which comes at the end of the festival of *Sukkot.*

The table on pp. 122-123 gives the Hebrew name of the *sidrah* (with a translation), then the biblical reference, and finally the *haftarah* text associated with the *sidrah.*

Weekly Bible Readings

		Torah	Prophets
1.	Bereshit (In the beginning)	Gen. 1:1—6:8	Isa. 42:5—43:11
2.	No'ach (Noah)	Gen. 6:9—11:32	Isa. 54:1—55:5
3.	Lekh Lekha (Go to!)	Gen. 12:1—17:27	Isa. 40:27—41:16
4.	Va-Yera (And he appeared)	Gen. 18:1—22:24	2 Kings 4:1-37
5.	Hayyei Sarah (Sarah lived)	Gen. 23:1—25:18	1 Kings 1:1-31
6.	Toledot (Descendants)	Gen. 25:19—28:9	Mal. 1:1—2:7
7.	Va-Yeze (And he left)	Gen. 28:10—32:3	Hos. 12:13—14:10
8.	Va-Yishlach (And he sent)	Gen. 32:4—36:43	Hos. 11:7—12:12
9.	Va-Yeshev (And he dwelt)	Gen. 37:1—40:23	Amos 2:6—3:8
10.	Mi-Kez (After)	Gen. 41:1—44:17	1 Kings 3:15—4:1
11.	Va-Yiggash (And he went up)	Gen. 44:18—47:27	Ezek. 37:15-28
12.	Va-Yechi (And he lived)	Gen. 47:28—50:26	1 Kings 2:1-12
13.	Shemot (Names)	Exod. 1:1—6:1	Isa. 27:6—28:13; 29:22-23
14.	Va-Era (And I appeared)	Exod. 6:2—9:35	Ezek. 28:25—29:21
15.	Bo (Go!)	Exod. 10:1—13:16	Jer. 46:13-28
16.	Be-Shallach (When he let go)	Exod. 13:17—17:16	Judg. 4:4—5:31
17.	Yitro (Jethro)	Exod. 18:1—20:23	Isa. 6:1—7:6; 9:5-6
18.	Mishpatim (Ordinances)	Exod. 21:1—24:18	Jer. 34:8-22; 33:25-26
19.	Terumah (Offering)	Exod. 25:1—27:19	1 Kings 5:26—6:13
20.	Tezavveh (You shall command)	Exod. 27:20—30:10	Ezek. 43:10-27
21.	Ki Tissa (When you take)	Exod. 30:11—34:35	1 Kings 18:1-39
22.	VaYakhel (And he assembled)	Exod. 35:1—38:20	1 Kings 7:40-50
23.	Pekudei (Sum)	Exod. 38:12—40:38	1 Kings 7:51—8:21
24.	Va-Yikra (And he called)	Lev. 1:1—5:26	Isa. 43:21—44:23
25.	Zav (Command!)	Lev. 6:1—8:26	Jer.7:21—8:3; 9:22-23
26.	Shemini (Eighth)	Lev. 9:1—11:47	2 Sam. 6:1—7:17
27.	Tazri'a (She conceives)	Lev. 12:1—13:59	2 Kings 4:42—5:19
28.	Mezora (Leper)	Lev. 14:1—15:33	2 Kings 7:3-20
29.	Acharei Mot (After the death)	Lev. 16:1—18:30	Ezek. 22:1-19
30.	Kedoshim (Holy)	Lev. 19:1—20:27	Amos 9:7-15
31.	Emor (Speak!)	Lev. 21:1—24:23	Ezek. 44:15-31
32.	Be-Har (On Mount)	Lev. 25:1—26:2	Jer. 32:6-27
33.	Be-Chukkotai (In my statutes)	Lev. 26:3—27:34	Jer. 16:19—17:14
34.	Be-Midbar (In the wilderness)	Num. 1:1—4:20	Hos. 2:1-22
35.	Naso (Take!)	Num. 4:21—7:89	Judg. 13:2-25
36.	Be-Ha'alotkha (When you set up)	Num. 8:1—12:16	Zech. 2:14—4:7
37.	Shelach Lekha (Send!)	Num. 13:1—15:41	Josh. 2:1-24
38.	Korach (Korah)	Num. 16:1—18:32	1 Sam. 11:14—12:22
39.	Chukat (Statute)	Num. 19:1—22:1	Judg. 11:1-33
40.	Balak (Balak)	Num. 22:2—25:9	Mic. 5:6—6:8
41.	Pinchas (Phinehas)	Num. 25:10—30:1	1 Kings 18:46—19:21
42.	Mattot (Tribes)	Num. 30:2—32:42	Jer. 1:1—2:3
43.	Masei (Stages)	Num. 33:1—36:13	Jer. 2:4-28; 3:4
44.	Devarim (Words)	Deut. 1:11—3:22	Isa. 1:1-27
45.	Va-Ethannan (And I besought)	Deut. 3:23—7:11	Isa. 40:1-26
46.	Ekev (Because)	Deut. 7:12—11:25	Isa. 49:14—51:3
47.	Re'eh (Behold!)	Deut. 11:26—16:17	Isa. 54:11—55:5
48.	Shofetim (Judges)	Deut. 16:18—21:9	Isa. 51:12—52:12

49. Ki Teze (When you go forth)	Deut. 21:10—25:19	Isa. 54:1-10
50. Ki Tavo (When you come)	Deut. 26:1—29:8	Isa. 60:1-22
51. Nizzavim (You stand)	Deut. 29:9—30:20	Isa. 61:10—63:9
52. Va-Yelekh (So he continued)	Deut. 31:1-30	Isa. 55:6—56:8
53. Ha'azinu (Give ear!)	Deut. 32:1-52	2 Sam. 22:1-51
54. Ve-Zot ha-Berakhah (And this is the blessing)	Deut. 33:1—34:12	Josh. 1:1-18

(Adapted from the *Encyclopaedia Judaica* 15:1249-1250)

PART FOUR

JEWISH TEACHINGS

13

The Content of Jewish Faith

The difference between the Christian faith and the Jewish faith has sometimes been summarized as follows: Christians are mainly concerned about doctrinal conformity and are less interested in agreement about right actions; Jews, however, are mainly interested in agreement about right actions but are not so concerned about uniformity in doctrine. This statement is an oversimplification, but it does contain a kernel of truth. Even the Talmud, the major source of postbiblical Jewish teachings, is mainly concerned with questions of behavior; books on systematic theology do not exist in Judaism. Nonetheless, there are clear conceptions of the content of the Jewish faith. Where is this faith expressed? What is the content of this faith? How is the Jewish confession of faith different from that of Christians?

Jewish Worship: Doctrine in Action

The content of Jewish faith is mediated to Jews in worship. This happens above all in prayer: "The Jew prays theology" (Jacob J. Petuchowski). Thus the Jewish Prayerbook, which transmits the rich prayer tradition of centuries virtually unchanged, also presents the essentials of Jewish doctrine. The one who calls on God in the words of this Prayerbook, whether in the synagogue worship service or at home, stands directly in the mainstream of Jewish doctrine and also gives witness to his or her own faith.

The festivals during the course of the year convey the strongest expressions of Jewish beliefs. In celebrating these festivals in the synagogue and at home, the mighty acts of God on behalf of God's people are remembered. These acts become both a personal experience of faith and the source of new hope. This is especially clear in the festival of Passover, in which the biblical experience of the people Israel (exodus, wilderness wandering, and entrance into the promised land) becomes the fundamental model for present-day faith: God delivers from affliction; God leads through times of distress; God keeps promises.

The Content of Jewish Faith

The most fundamental statement of Jewish faith is the confession of faith in the one God, the God of Israel. In daily prayer each morning and evening and in the last hour of life, every Jew is supposed to pray that confession in the words of the *Shema:* "Hear, O Israel, the Lord is our God, the Lord is one" (Deut. 6:4). In this way the *Shema* comes very close to what Christians understand as a confession of faith.

But Jewish faith can also express itself in the fullness of the entire prayer tradition as found in the Jewish Prayerbook, such as in the biblical Psalms, the *Amidah* (see pp. 86-89), or the *Kaddish*.

The necessity for a concise and memorable summary of Jewish faith came up time and again in the Diaspora, as Jews encountered and entered into debate with their non-Jewish environment. The 13 articles of the creed of the famous Jewish scholar Moses Maimonides (1135–1204) attained the greatest importance. These are formulated in a manner corresponding to Christian and Islamic confessions of faith:

I believe . . .

1. That God alone is the Creator.
2. That He is absolutely One.
3. That He has no body or bodily shape.
4. That He is the first and the last.
5. That only to Him may we pray and to no other.
6. That the words of the Prophets are true.
7. That the prophecy of Moses is true, and that he is the father of all prophets.
8. That the Torah, now found in our hands, was given to Moses.
9. That this Torah is not subject to change, and that there will never be another Torah from the Creator.
10. That the Creator knows all the thoughts and deeds of man.
11. That He rewards and punishes according to the deed.
12. That the Messiah will come; though he tarry, I will expect him daily.
13. That the dead will be resurrected.

(*Judaism: Development and Life* by Leo Trepp, Wadsworth, 1982, p. 63.)

The confessional statements written by Maimonides have been incorporated into the Jewish Prayerbook and have thus gained the widest recognition. Nevertheless, they have never been declared a binding confession for all of Judaism. It is not necessary for an individual Jew to subscribe to every detail of these assertions.

Joseph Albo (1380–1444) formulated an even more concise summary of the Jewish faith, which he wished to set alongside the confessions of Christianity and

Islam: "The three fundamentals of Israelite religion are the three truths in which the Israelite must believe: the belief in the existence of the one, the only highest God, the belief that the Torah was given to us directly from God and the belief that God is a righteous Judge, who rewards and punishes human beings according to their actions."

Jewish and Christian Confessions of Faith

The Jewish confession of faith has its setting in the worship service and continues into daily life, in which the will of God as revealed in the Torah is put into practice. This includes the readiness to be a witness for God before the world, as well as readiness for martyrdom, called *Kiddush Hashem* (sanctification of God's name).

While the individual Jew enjoys a great deal of freedom in the formulation of his or her faith, much care is given to formulating specific guidelines for conduct—especially in Orthodox Judaism. The Torah provides the guidelines for witnessing to the faith in both word and deed.

Christian witness is also rooted in worship and finds its continuation in service to God in everyday life. Christians, also, are to be ready to confess their faith in the presence of any person. In recent times, however, Christians have suffered far less than Jews have.

In working out Christian conduct, with the Ten Commandments as the basis, Christians are given a great deal of freedom for individual decision and responsibility before God. However, Christians take great pains in formulating their confessions of faith, to which differing accents are given by various denominations. The center of the faith, uniting all Christians, is Jesus Christ, whom all Christians confess to be the Mediator between the one God and humankind.

14

The Pharisees

In popular opinion, a Pharisee is a self-righteous hypocrite. When the New Testament is read in a worship service and Pharisees are mentioned without further explanation, this caricature is associated with Jews. The most well-known example is the parable of the Pharisee and the tax collector (Luke 18:9-14). This picture of the Pharisees does an injustice to Jews in general and to the Pharisees in particular. It is important for Christians to have an accurate understanding of the Pharisees.

The Pharisees in Jewish History

The Pharisees were a religious lay movement within Judaism. Little is known about their beginnings. We have historical evidence that they were in existence as an organized religious group by the end of the second century before Christ. Their goal was to lead exemplary lives according to the Torah. In everyday life they tried to follow biblical directives that had been intended only for priests: they avoided contact with any expression of Gentile religion and also kept their distance from anyone among their own people who did not take the Torah as seriously as they did. They understood the Torah not just according to its literal meaning, but also according to their own system of scriptural interpretation.

The name *Pharisees* (from the Hebrew *perushim,* meaning "separated ones") most likely refers to their separation from those who were uneducated as well as to their separate interpretation of Scripture. They were soon recognized as teachers of the people and as spiritual leaders within Judaism. They were the first Jewish teachers to state clearly that there would be a resurrection of the dead. The Pharisees and the scribes were the forerunners of the rabbis.

In contrast to the situation in the Diaspora outside of Israel or to that in Galilee, the Pharisees in Jerusalem at the time of Jesus were an important political force. The Jewish political authorities had varied opinions of them. Herod the Great, for example, treated them with well-intended neutrality. Since most Pharisees had hopes for Israel's future in terms of direct intervention from God rather than in military or political achievements, he saw nothing suspicious about them.

Judaism at that time (above all, the dominating group of Sadducees) nevertheless considered the Pharisees to be dangerous, because they added their own oral interpretation to the written Torah and were determined advocates of this interpretation. Several "schools" and movements arose among the Pharisees: the school of Shammai interpreted the Torah with the greatest possible strictness, while the school of Hillel offered interpretations which were more open and charitable. The efforts of the Pharisees to shape the whole of life according to God's commandments were sincere; they were convinced that any devout person was obligated to fulfill the Torah to the greatest degree possible. Paul acknowledged his own background as a Pharisee (Phil. 3:5).

After the destruction of Jerusalem and the temple in the year A.D. 70, the Sadducees and radical nationalistic groups such as the Zealots disappeared. This was the decisive historical opportunity for the Pharisees. They now became the most important bearers of Israel's religious convictions. They stood for the consecration of everyday life through complete obedience to the Torah. They also advocated making peace with the governing authorities, as long as they did not prevent them from carrying out their religious obligations. From their spiritual and intellectual center in Jamnia, the Pharisees gave Judaism a new social and individual order, based primarily on the school of Hillel. It was under their leadership that rabbinic Judaism developed. They established the canon of Old Testament scriptures and gave the synagogue the function and meaning which it has to this day.

The Pharisees in the New Testament

The Pharisees are mentioned about 100 times in the New Testament, most often in the Gospels. They are portrayed in very different ways.

Luke reports that Jesus had table fellowship with the Pharisees. He also mentions that at the time of Jesus, discussions concerning fundamental issues were going on within Pharisaism. John names particular Pharisees as good discussion partners with Jesus. The book of Acts reports several instances of support for the apostles from the Pharisees, and also the belief in the resurrection of the dead which was common to Pharisees and Christians (Acts 5:34-39; 23:6-9).

It is interesting to see how the question about the most important commandment is handled (Mark 12:28-33; Luke 10:25-28; Matt. 22:34-40). In Mark and Luke, the scribe (who asks the question) and Jesus (who answers it) come to an agreement with one another. In Matthew, the question already appears as a conscious confrontation and provocation by a Pharisee, and not a word is said about an agreement. Matthew generally pictures the Pharisees as a group of Jews who are hostile to Jesus.

The Gospels state that the Pharisees plotted against Jesus, and that there were severe conflicts between Jesus and the Pharisees. This way of presenting things may be related to the fact that at the time when the Gospels were composed, Judaism was increasingly being represented by the Pharisees.

According to the witness of the Gospels, Jesus was not continuously in dispute with the Pharisees. He also had conflicts with other groups. What part did the differences between the Pharisees and Jesus on the interpretation of Scripture play in the sentencing of Jesus? The New Testament witness is not clear on this question. From the viewpoint of the period after A.D. 70, the "Pharisees and scribes" could have appeared to the editors of the Gospels as the representatives of all of Judaism; perhaps for this reason, the conflicts which Jesus had with them were stressed.

Later on, the church saw the Jews—especially the Pharisees—as the enemies of Jesus, and all the more distorted and caricatured the picture of the Pharisees as hypocrites.

A Job to Be Done

The historical effects of this picture of the Pharisees have been far-reaching. In the pre-Reformation period, the polemic against the Pharisees was tied up with the general anti-Jewish attitude. When the Bible began to be read in the language of the people in the churches of the Reformation, the caricature of the Pharisees became widespread and eventually even proverbial.

English dictionaries offer the following meanings for "pharisaic" or "pharisaical": "Observing the form, but neglecting the spirit, of religion; self-righteous; hypocritical" (Funk and Wagnalls, 1954); "making an outward show of piety and morality but lacking the inward spirit; censorious of others' morals or practices; formal, sanctimonious, self-righteous, hypocritical" (Webster's 3rd, 1961); "hypocritical, canting, pecksniffian, pharisaical, sanctimonious, self-righteous" (Webster's Collegiate Thesaurus, 1976); "Of or practicing hypocrisy" (Roget's II: The New Thesaurus, 1980).

These dictionaries do not all mention the origin of the term *Pharisee*. But most people know that the word has something to do with Jews. In any case, awareness of the original religious meaning of the concept is disappearing more and more from today's biblically illiterate society.

What should be done about this widespread distortion of the picture of the Pharisee and the anti-Jewish attitude that goes with it? Christians have the job of examining their use of language. And here is another matter for Christians to think about: the term *Christian* often has the same negative ring for Jews as *Pharisee* does for Christians. Because of the painful experiences Jews have had, the word *Christian* is easily associated with arrogance and with a contradiction between one's words and actions.

The term *Pharisee* should therefore be used only in its historical sense, within the context of Judaism of the biblical period. We should weigh our words carefully, on the one hand recognizing the sincere efforts of the Pharisees in response to God's grace, and on the other hand evaluating the criticism which the Christian faith has made of Pharisaism. The meaning of the parable of the Pharisee and the tax collector is that each—like every person—is judged to be righteous before God only by God's grace.

We need to guard against the thoughtless use of the words *Pharisee* and *pharisaic* in everyday language, since such usage simply perpetuates anti-Jewish prejudice. In sermons, Bible studies, and religious instruction, we should take special care with those passages from the Gospels which, mostly because of their usual interpretation, have given rise to a distorted or caricatured picture of the Pharisees. These biblical passages need to be correctly explained by a precise description of the actual history of the Pharisee movement. Such a careful and corrected use of the term *Pharisee* will indicate a willingness to overcome such thoughtless anti-Jewish attitudes.

15

The Talmud

Next to the Hebrew Bible (the "Old Testament," as Christians call it), the Talmud is one of the most important writings for Jews. The Talmud is a collection of Jewish oral tradition.

Many Christians have heard of the Talmud. But few know what it contains and what to think of it. What significance does the Talmud have? Where did it come from? A response to these questions needs to begin with the revelation of God at Mount Sinai.

God's Instruction for Israel: The Torah

After the people of Israel had been freed from Egyptian bondage, they received the Torah on Sinai, the mountain of God's revelation. In the Torah (which means "instruction" or "teaching"), God's will for Israel is explained. God's will is expressed more concisely in the Ten Commandments (Exodus 20), and then in an expanded manner in the 603 additional "obligations" in the Pentateuch (Genesis through Deuteronomy). The purpose of all these regulations was that God's will would be respected and put into practice in life. Eventually the first five books of the Hebrew Bible became known as "Torah."

The people of Israel received the Torah of God through Moses; this is one of the central assertions of Jewish faith. Israel pledged its loyalty to the Torah and promised to live by it (Exod. 19:8; 24:3). Israel has gone through history with the Torah; the people have found joy in the Torah and have held onto it even in times of suffering. The goal of this journey is the redemption which will come in the days when messianic salvation begins for Israel and for the world. The Jewish Prayerbook says:

> Praised are You, Lord our God, King of the universe who has chosen us from among all peoples by giving us His Torah. . . .
> This is the life style for Torah students:
> Eat a salty crust of bread, ration your drinking water,
> Sleep on the ground, live a life of privation,
> Exhaust yourself in Torah study.
> If you live in this manner, "You will be happy and all will go well with you" (Psalm 128:2). "You will be happy" in this world; "all will go well with you" in the world-to-come.

(*Siddur Sim Shalom: A Prayerbook for Shabbat, Festivals, and Weekdays,* pp. 569, 657.)

In the course of a year, the whole Torah is read on Sabbath days in the synagogue, section by section. The Torah is represented visually in the synagogue by the two tables of the law as well as by a crown.

The Oral Torah

The first five books of the Hebrew Bible are called "written Torah." According to a widespread view, there has also existed from the beginning an "oral Torah." This was formulated whenever new circumstances demanded it. For example, after the Jerusalem temple had been destroyed, worship had to be handled in a new way. This "oral Torah" is also said to have been given to Moses on Sinai, and in this way it receives its authority.

A group of professional scribes developed, whose job it was to explain the Torah and make it available to each generation. The scribes were the teachers (*rabbis*) of Israel. In houses of study, decisions were made about the application of Torah to life.

The Formation of the Talmud

After the destruction of the Jerusalem temple in the catastrophe of A.D. 70, when most Jews had to live among foreigners, the cohesiveness and the traditions of the people became endangered. In response to this situation the teachers of Israel decided to put into writing the oral Torah as it had developed up to that time. So at the end of the second century, the *Mishnah* (from the Hebrew *shanah*, "to repeat," in the sense of learning by memory) was formed. One of the teachers who worked on the collection of the *Mishnah* was Gamaliel the First, the teacher of the apostle Paul. With its 63 Tractates (lessons) in six Orders, the *Mishnah* specifies for devout Jews the manner and direction of their lives, actions, and thoughts.

In the course of its historical development, the *Mishnah* also had to be commented on, because new decisions had to be made. These commentaries contained debates about the content of the *Mishnah*, giving arguments both pro and con. At times these arguments conclude with decisions; at times the discussion is left open. They were put into written form at the end of the fifth century and were added to the *Mishnah* as *Gemara* (from the Hebrew *gamar*, "complete"; that is, the completion of the *Mishnah* in the sense of explanation and interpretation). *Mishnah* and *Gemara* together make up the Talmud, which corresponds to the English word "teaching."

There are two Talmuds, because the *Gemara,* which came from the houses of study in Galilee, in the land of Israel, developed differently there than it did in the Diaspora. The Palestinian Talmud (called the Jerusalem Talmud) was completed in the fourth century. The Talmud which grew up in the Diaspora (called the Babylonian Talmud) was completed somewhat later, in the sixth century. This Babylonian Talmud became authoritative in later times for decisions about correct teaching. It is three or four times longer than the Jerusalem Talmud.

As time went on, the Talmud also needed to be explained, and this explanation took the form of commentaries. Alongside these there were also attempts to collect the most important decisions about teachings; the most well-known handbook is the *Shulhan Arukh* ("the well-prepared table," after Ps. 23:5a), written by Joseph Karo in 1564–1565.

Living with the Talmud

"Talmud Torah" means not only the study of the Torah, but also the way of life of the Jew. To teach and to learn Torah is always required. Regular study of Talmud, either individually or in a group, goes along with this. For religiously liberal Jews, the Talmud does not have the same central significance that it does for Orthodox Jews.

The way of life which the Talmud portrays is described in various ways. The *Halakhah* (from the Hebrew *halak,* "to go" or "to walk") describes the legal side of life. All Talmudic sayings which give binding directions about actions may be called *Halakhah*. The nonlegal parts of the Talmud are called *Haggadah* (from *higgid*, "to tell"). In this category are stories which, often in an embellished manner, aim to encourage one to do the right thing.

The Talmud—Misunderstood and Misinterpreted

Though Jews and Christians have lived together for centuries, most Christians have no knowledge whatsoever of the Talmud. It has often been considered a secretive book that contains things not only strange and difficult to understand, but also dangerous to Christianity. Because of this, sharp suspicions concerning the Talmud have often been voiced within Christianity. The Talmud and other Jewish literature have been declared "forbidden books," and there were even times when Jews were forced to hand them over to be burned. In the face of all this, it is almost a miracle that a number of valuable manuscripts of the Talmud from early times have survived. A complete manuscript of the Babylonian Talmud—written in 1343—can be found in Munich.

The Talmud and Christians Today

In the New Testament one can find examples of Talmud-like interpretation of Scripture, such as Jesus' interpretation of the commandment about divorce (Matt. 19:1-12; Mark 10:1-12) or Paul's explanation of the two sons of Abraham in terms of bondage and freedom (Gal. 4:21-31). In such portions of the New Testament, as well as in many parts of the Old Testament, Christians can see ways of dealing with earlier expressions of God's will which are very similar to those found in the Talmud.

When Christians later forgot or denied their own faith's connection with the Jews, the attitude of the church toward Jews became unfaithful to itself. This attitude opened the door to anti-Semitism and resulted in a long history of persecution of the Jews, for which the church must acknowledge its guilt.

Although there are deep-seated differences between what Christians and Jews believe, they can encounter one another with respect and understanding. If Christians today give the Talmud a candid hearing, they will gain great respect for it and for the sincerity of Israel's teachers, who attempted to direct all of life according to the will of God.

The reproduction on page 143 shows the first page of the standard edition of the Babylonian Talmud with the beginning of the Tractate *Berakhot* (Blessings). The Talmud text is in the middle column. Directly under the first word, printed in large type, is the *Mishnah*. Beginning in the middle of this column, recognizable by the two letters printed in larger type, is the *Gemara*. To the left of the text of the Talmud is the commentary of Rashi (abbreviation for *Ra*bbi *Sh*lomo ben *I*saac, 1040–1105, of France), the most important Talmudic interpreter of the Middle Ages. To the right of the Talmud text are comments from the school of Rashi. On the extreme left border in smaller print are other commentaries. The way in which the Talmud is printed illustrates the gradual growth of the traditional material.

Excerpt from a Rabbinical Discussion in the Talmud

In Section 1:1 of the Tractate *Berakhot*, the discussion concerns the question of how late in the evening one

מאימתי

A page from the Babylonian Talmud.

can postpone the obligation to pray the *Shema Israel*. Rabbi Eliezer thinks one can wait until the end of the first night watch; the "wise," that is, the teachers of the *Mishnah*, say until midnight; Rabbi Gamaliel says, until the dawn breaks. The question is left open in the *Mishnah* and the *Gemara* attempts to clarify the matter:

Whose view did the Sages adopt? If it is R. Eliezer's view, then let them express themselves in the same way as R. Eliezer? If it is R. Gamaliel's view, let them express themselves in the same way as R. Gamaliel?—In reality it is R. Gamaliel's view that they adopted, and their reason for saying, UNTIL MIDNIGHT is to keep a man far from transgression. For so it has been taught: The Sages made a fence for their words so that a man, on returning home from the field in the evening, should not say: I shall go home, eat a little, drink a little, sleep a little, and then I shall recite the *Shema'* and the *Tefillah,* and meanwhile, sleep may overpower him, and as a result he will sleep the whole night. Rather should a man, when returning home from the field in the evening, go to the synagogue. If he is used to read the Bible, let him read the Bible, and if he is used to repeat the Mishnah, let him repeat the Mishnah, and then let him recite the *Shema'* and say the *Tefillah,* [go home] and eat his meal and say the Grace.

(*The Babylonian Talmud: Seder Zera' im,* trans. and ed. Rabbi Dr. I. Epstein, The Soncino Press, 1948, pp. 12-13.)

Excerpt from the Teachings of the Sages (Pirkei Avot)

The basic declarations about the unbroken chain of bearers of the tradition—from the reception of Torah (instruction) on Sinai by Moses and on—is found in the beginning of the Tractate *Pirkei Avot* (Teachings of the Sages; 300 B.C.–A.D. 200) in the Babylonian Talmud:

Moses received Torah from God at Sinai.
He transmitted it to Joshua,
Joshua to the Elders, the Elders to the Prophets,
the Prophets to the members of the Great Assembly.

They formulated three precepts:

Be cautious in rendering a decision,
Rear many students,
Build a fence to protect Torah.

Shimon Ha-Tzaddik was one of the last members of the Great Assembly. This was a favorite teaching of his:

The world rests on three things—
on Torah, on service of God, on deeds of love.

Antigonus, of Sokho, received the tradition from Shimon Ha-Tzaddik. This was a favorite teaching of his:

Do not be like servants who serve their master expecting to receive a reward; be rather like servants who serve their master unconditionally, with no thought of reward. Also, let the fear of God determine your actions.

Hillel taught:
Do not withdraw from the community;
Do not be sure of yourself till the day of your death;
Do not judge your fellow human being till you stand in his situation;
Do not say "It is not possible to understand this," for ultimately it will be understood;
Do not say "When I have leisure, I will study," for you may never have leisure.

This was a favorite teaching of his:
A boor cannot be reverent;
An ignoramus cannot be pious;
A shy person cannot learn;
An ill-tempered person cannot teach;
Not everyone engrossed in business learns wisdom;
Where there are no worthy persons, strive to be a worthy person.

(*Siddur Sim Shalom: A Prayerbook for Shabbat, Festivals, and Weekdays,* pp. 603, 613, translated by Rabbi Max J. Routtenberg.)

16

Messianic Expectation

The expectation of the Messiah, who will deliver Israel and the nations from all the troubles of this world, has been a part of Jewish faith since biblical times. The word *Messiah* is derived from the Hebrew *mashiah,* "the anointed one," originally a designation for the ruling king. (The word *Christ* is derived from *christos,* the Greek translation of *mashiah.*)

The 12th article of the 13 articles of faith by the Jewish scholar Maimonides (1135–1204) says: "I believe that the Messiah will come; though he tarry, I will expect him daily." Similarly, the Jewish Prayerbook says: "At the end of days he will send our anointed, to deliver those who wait for the final deliverance." What will the Messiah bring? In what form will the Messiah come, and what phenomena will accompany the Messiah's coming? How does the messianic age relate to the end of history? How are Christian and Jewish messianic expectations different? These questions will be dealt with in this chapter.

The Work of the Messiah

Jewish messianic expectation is based on the biblical message, the witness to God's history with this world. God, the Creator of the world, will also determine its end. This end does not mean chaos or destruction, but rather salvation for the people of Israel and for all peoples. The task of the people of Israel is, by its very existence, to be a witness to the world that Israel is moving toward this God-given salvation. To hold on to this hope is Israel's destiny.

The Messiah, Israel's promised king of the end time, will usher in the time of salvation. With the Messiah's coming, the final and complete rule of God (the kingdom of God, kingdom of heaven, or rule of heaven), which includes all areas of life, breaks into this world. Those who submit to the "yoke of the Torah" and who therefore seek to do God's will in their lives and among their people find themselves in the kingdom of God. Those who allow themselves to be ruled by God in this way, and who acknowledge God's rule over their lives, belong to the true Israel.

The task of the coming Messiah is the complete establishment of God's rule, not only in Israel, but also among the nations. Then the people Israel will be delivered from suffering and oppression caused by other nations; all persecution, degradation, and contempt will cease, and Israel will find its rightful place in this world.

"Deliverance" in this context does not mean so much deliverance from sin and guilt as national liberation. At that time there will be peace (*shalom,* in the sense of total well-being) for Israel and for all nations. The Jewish understanding of deliverance and peace has to do with this world, with the whole world. Every messianic claim will be measured by whether it brings this kind of worldwide peace. When the Messiah has brought this peace of God into the world, then the Messiah's task is finished, and God will be king: "And the Lord will become king over all the earth; on that day the Lord will be one and his name one" (Zech. 14:9).

The Time and the Person of the Messiah

Since biblical times, Israel has expected deliverance to come in a period when the people would be experiencing especially great oppression. The greatness of the one whom God will use as rescuer and deliverer, the Messiah, will correspond to the greatness of the suffering. This will be the time of the "messianic woes."

For this reason, expectations of messianic deliverance have been especially strong in times of great national suffering. In the time after the destruction of the Jerusalem temple by the Romans, many Jews set their hopes on Bar Kochba, a freedom fighter in whom they thought they recognized the Messiah. His three-year fight for liberation, understood by many as the "final battle," ended in A.D. 135 in a terrible defeat for the Jewish people.

In the 17th century, under the pressure of horrible persecutions in Eastern Europe, Sabbatai Zevi presented himself as Messiah. But then, in what was supposed to be the messianic year of 1666, as a Turkish prisoner he was forced to convert to Islam. This resulted in deep disappointment and disillusionment on the part of his many followers.

Impressed by such experiences, Jewish teachers emphasized more and more that the coming of the Messiah was not so much dependent on national disaster as on the faith and piety of the people: "If Israel keeps only one Sabbath exactly as it should be kept, then the Messiah will come." Also, statements about the form in which the Messiah would come became more and more cautious.

The Bible itself gives a variety of answers to questions about the who and the how of the Messiah. According to Dan. 7:13-14, a Messiah is expected who will step into his God-given royal office in victorious and radiant glory; according to Zech. 9:9, the Messiah is a king who will begin his work in deep humility. These contradictory pictures eventually led to the expectation of two messianic figures who would appear one after the other, in the end time; one as a son of David, the prototype of Israel's kings, and the other as a son of Joseph, or Ephraim. The son of Joseph would die in the battle with Israel's enemies, and the son of David would lead to victory and to messianic deliverance. These conceptions, however, claimed no ultimate authority.

The long path of Israel's history and the numerous disappointed messianic hopes have led some contemporary Jews to transfer their expectations for the Messiah from an individual to the entire Jewish people: Israel as a whole is seen as the fulfillment of the ancient, messianic hope. In modern times many Jews, filled with Zionistic ideals, have directed their hopes toward a State of Israel which could be a model for the world; a state where Jews would not suffer as they did when they lived among the nations, and where justice and peace would rule. Despite the differences in messianic concepts, the coming of messianic salvation as a hope of Israel continues to be a focus for Jewish prayer, not only in the worship of the congregation, but also in the daily prayer of the individual: "May the merciful God make us worthy of the days of the Messiah and the life of the world to come. . . ."

The Messianic Age and the World to Come

The goal of Israel's hope is the world to come, which will be ushered in by the coming of the Messiah. The transition from the one world to the other will be gradual; a strict separation is not possible. The resurrection of the dead also belongs to the renewal of the world, which begins with the Messiah's coming. A prayer to be used at burial says: "God's great name will be exalted and sanctified in the world which will one day be made new. He restores the dead to life and leads them to eternal life. He builds the city of Jerusalem and crowns his temple in it. He removes idolatry from the earth and restores the worship of heaven to its place again [that is, on earth!]. [Then] the Holy One will rule, praised be he, in his kingdom and in his splendor. . . ."

The world, which will be renewed after the Messiah has come, will experience divine salvation: a time of deliverance, peace, good fortune, God's favor and mercy, and life with God. There will be no more sickness, hunger, need, misery, or death in the world to come. Of that world it is said: "Except for you, O God, no eye has seen it." For this reason it is not proper for human beings to develop concepts and pictures of God's new world.

Christian and Jewish Expectations

Christians and Jews share the hope for a future time of salvation which will not be brought about by human programs or teachings. The world does not merely require renewal by its own resources, but rather a new creation brought about by God, the Creator.

But Christian and Jewish ideas about the Messiah have gone their separate ways. For believing Jews, the Sabbath with its Sabbath rest is an anticipation of the coming messianic time of salvation. For believing Christians, life with Jesus Christ is already a part of the new creation (through a new birth), an anticipation of the coming time of salvation. Christians believe that in Jesus of Nazareth, the Messiah (the Christ) has come as the sacrifice and offer of salvation for Israel and the whole world. They await the return of Jesus Christ in the last days.

PART FIVE

JESUS

17

The Old Testament:
Jewish Book
and Christian Book

Both Christians and Jews claim the Bible as their authority. But the Bible is not the same for both. For Christians, the Bible—the Holy Scripture—consists of the "Old" and the "New" Testaments. For Jews, however, the Bible or Holy Scripture is only the first of these two parts. Christians added the "New Testament" and renamed the first part the "Old Testament." Because both Jews and Christians count it as the Bible, the Old Testament is the most important link between the two communities.

The Book of the Jews

The words of the Old Testament are the same for both Jews and Christians. But there are some differences in the order of the individual books. The Jewish arrangement is:

- the five books of Moses, together called the *Torah,* that is, "instruction" or "law": Genesis, Exodus, Leviticus, Numbers, and Deuteronomy.
- the *Prophets,* including:
  the "former prophets": Joshua, Judges, 1 and 2 Samuel, and 1 and 2 Kings; and
  the "latter prophets": Isaiah, Jeremiah, Ezekiel, the Book of the Twelve (Hosea, Joel, Amos, Obadiah, Jonah, Micah, Nahum, Habakkuk, Zephaniah, Haggai, Zechariah, and Malachi).

• The *Writings:* the Psalms, Job, Proverbs, Ruth, Song of Solomon, Lamentations, Esther, Daniel, Ezra, Nehemiah, and 1 and 2 Chronicles.

Jews usually call the Old Testament the *Tenakh,* an acronymn formed from the Hebrew names for each section: *Torah, Nebi'im.* (Prophets) and *Ketubim* (Writings).

For Jews, these three parts of the Bible do not have the same status. "Moses received the Torah on Sinai and passed it on. . . ." This sentence from Jewish tradition expresses the fact that Judaism sees the Torah as the fundamental revelation. All further revelation and scriptural interpretation—oral or written—is related to and measured by the event on Sinai. Therefore, the five books of Moses (Genesis, Exodus, Leviticus, Numbers, and Deuteronomy) carry the most weight for Jews; they report the revelation at Sinai.

The language of the Old Testament is Hebrew or, in a few sections, Aramaic, the language spoken at the time of Jesus. For this reason it is referred to as the "Hebrew Bible." Even before the time of Christ, it was translated into Greek, the common language of the time. The books of the New Testament were first written in Greek, not Hebrew.

The Book of Jesus and the First Christians

The Old Testament (as it was later named) was the Bible of Jesus and the first Christian congregations. The story of Jesus in the temple at the age of 12 shows that Jesus had been familiar with the Bible since childhood (Luke 2:41-52). He was brought up in the tradition of the Torah (Gal. 4:4). On the cross he prayed words from the Psalms. Time and again he referred to

"Moses and the prophets" (see Luke 16:31), that is, to "the Scriptures." He understood himself as the one who fulfilled the words of the prophets: "Today this Scripture has been fulfilled in your hearing" (Luke 4:21).

The first Christian congregations were made up of Jews who confessed Jesus to be the Messiah, the Christ. To the "law and the prophets" (Matt. 22:40) they added the account of the revelation of the crucified and risen Messiah who would one day return. Believing that Jesus was Lord, they gained a new understanding of the Scriptures. They found the work of Jesus already sketched out in the Old Testament and in it also discovered how their own lives and work fit into God's plan.

Disputes with the larger portion of Judaism that did not believe in Jesus did not lead these first Christians to oppose the Old Testament. On the contrary: since they believed that Jesus had fulfilled the Scriptures, they could claim to be the first to understand them in their fullness.

With such a claim, conflict with the Jewish teachers was unavoidable. These teachers understood the Bible primarily as *instruction* for the lives of God's people, but for the Christians, the *prophecy* fulfilled in Jesus the Messiah was the essential key for scriptural interpretation. The Christian community quickly expanded beyond the confines of the Jewish people, and the message of the Christians was rejected by the majority of the Jews as being alien to Judaism. The church eventually gathered up some of its own writings as a "New Testament" and made it authoritative for Christians.

Jewish Book and Christian Book

Because Christians read the same Scriptures that Jews read, neither group can be indifferent to the way in which the other interprets them. In the past, the opposition between Christians and Jews was emphasized. In the Christian view, Jewish interpretations of the Old Testament were inadequate because they did not consider the decisive saving event which took place in Jesus Christ. Jewish interpretations were either opposed or ignored. This even led to a devaluation of the entire Old Testament in comparison with the New.

For example, the Old Testament was sometimes considered as a document of revelation only for Judaism, and the New Testament alone was seen as a revelatory document for Christianity. It was said that the Old Testament contained only questions and the New Testament the answer; or that the Old had only the law, the New the gospel; or the Old had only promise, the New the fulfillment. Eventually the Old Testament was considered as "old" and outdated, while only the New Testament was understood as forever valid and "new."

For Jews, the Hebrew Bible remained the basis for teaching and worship through the centuries. The preservation of the Jewish faith in the face of persecution, and the revival of Hebrew language and culture in the State of Israel cannot be understood without the Bible. The profound experiences which Jews have had with the Bible throughout the course of history are once again being taken into consideration by Christian interpreters. These experiences could contribute to a completely new consciousness in the church. The contemporary interchange with Jewish biblical interpretation also leads to a new consideration of the fundamental questions of the Christian faith: Is Jesus the promised Messiah? Do we have access to God through him alone? Does Jesus also fulfill the hope of the Jews? The new Jewish interest in the figure of Jesus can contribute to a better understanding of both the Jewish background of the New Testament and the unity of the entire Scripture.

The Book of the Church

Despite all tendencies to the contrary, Christianity has time and again reached the conclusion that the Old Testament remains an indispensable part of the Holy Scriptures. The Old and New Testaments form an inseparable unity and tell one story: the story of God with humanity. The Bible tells how the one God created and preserves this world and its one people, how these people rebel against their Creator, and how God leads those who have fallen away back once again. The special story of redemption begins with Abraham, in whom "all the families of the earth shall be blessed" (Gen. 12:3), and leads up to Jesus Christ.

So there is an arc which stretches from the first to the last pages of the Bible. The New Testament cannot be understood without the Old. It always presupposes what the Old Testament says about God's action in creation, about the life-embracing experience of God's blessing, about God's peace and salvation, and about the directives for a responsible life before God.

For Christians, the message of the Bible is disclosed in the revelation of the one God through Jesus Christ. The ongoing task of Christians is to transplant the message of the whole Bible into the reality of life. Precisely for this reason it is important that the Old Testament continue to be a book for Christians as well as for

Jews. Through this book the church is kept pointed toward the people of Israel. By taking seriously God's ways with these people, the church will rightly recognize its own calling.

Excerpt from a Jewish Song at Simhat Torah

The following is an excerpt from a Jewish song that has been sung since the 11th century as part of the Simhat Torah festival.

I am joyously happy on Simchat Torah.
May God's servant, the Branch, come on Simchat Torah.
Our Torah is for all a tree of life;
From Thee is this source of all life.
Abraham rejoiced on Simchat Torah;
Isaac rejoiced on Simchat Torah;
Jacob rejoiced on Simchat Torah;
Moses, Aaron rejoiced on Simchat Torah;
Joshua, Samuel rejoiced on Simchat Torah;
David, Solomon rejoiced on Simchat Torah;
Our Torah is for all a tree of life.
From Thee is this source of all life.

(*The Traditional Prayer Book for Sabbath and Festivals,* ed. and trans. David de sola Pool, University Books, 1960, p. 584.)

18

Jesus the Jew

Many Christians are not aware that Jesus was a Jew, that he lived his entire life within first-century Judaism, and that they already have a connection to the Jews because of this fact. Most often, Christians have sub-consciously thought of Jesus as a Christian. Even Jews have frequently considered Jesus a Christian. Only in recent times have large numbers of both Christians and Jews begun to recognize that Jesus is firmly anchored in Judaism. Jesus was a Jew, but his significance—at least for Christians—goes far beyond that.

Jesus—Born and Brought Up As a Jew

The New Testament describes Jesus as a Jew, "born of [a Jewish] woman, born under the law [instructed in the Torah]" (Gal. 4:4). The stories preceding his birth and those about his childhood describe him as a Jewish child, born in Bethlehem, the city of King David. Jesus' parents are described as devout Jews who observed the commandments of the Jewish faith in raising their child. Through circumcision, Jesus was included in the covenant with Abraham and made a member of the Jewish people and community of faith. The story about the 12-year-old Jesus in the temple may be a reference to an early form of the Bar Mitzvah celebration. Jesus was therefore obligated to live by the Torah of Israel, to keep its commandments and to "fulfill" the will of God revealed in it (Matt. 5:17).

Jesus had a comprehensive knowledge of the biblical tradition. Young Jews learned how to read and write with the help of the Scriptures of the Old Testament in schools affiliated with the synagogues. They also learned how to pray there and were instructed in the history of Israel and in the "oral Torah."

Jesus—a Teacher of Israel

As an adult, Jesus was a teacher both in the synagogues and in public, and was accordingly addressed as "Rabbi." Jesus' teaching was not directed against the Jewish faith as the Torah presented that faith. For Jesus, the will of God revealed in the Torah was binding (Matt. 5:17-19). In the same manner as the school of the renowned Pharisaic teacher Hillel, Jesus opposed those teachers of Israel (such as the Pharisaic school of Shammai) who imposed an almost unbearable burden on their people with the rigidity of their interpretation of Torah.

Jesus' Sermon on the Mount (Matthew 5–7) reflects the teaching methods of the established teachers of the Talmud. The Beatitudes have parallels in the Old Testament and in rabbinic writings. The parables of Jesus, in which religious and ethical ideas and demands are made clear through the use of a comparison (Hebrew, *mashal*), have many similarities with the rabbinic teaching tradition. Thus Jesus did not take a position fundamentally opposed to the Pharisees and their method of teaching. Even some Jewish scholars see Jesus as a Jew who was faithful to the Torah.

We can imagine Jesus as a Jew of his time, with tassels on the four corners of his outer garment and wearing phylacteries at daily prayer. In accord with the biblical directives, he regularly went to Jerusalem for the great pilgrimage festivals—Passover, *Shavuot,* and *Sukkot*. He celebrated the Passover with his disciples and observed the dietary laws. He ordered a healed leper to make the prescribed sacrifice and to present himself to the priests for verification of the healing. He understood his mission primarily as one to the Jewish people, though he did not exclude either Samaritans or Gentiles on principle.

One cannot conclude from the New Testament that Jesus, who went to the synagogue on the Sabbath according to Jewish tradition (Luke 4:16), disregarded the Sabbath laws. The Torah seeks to protect and support human life (Lev. 18:5). Though keeping the Sabbath is one of its central commandments, according to Jesus, the Sabbath was made for people, and not the other way around. The Talmud, also, places the protection of life above all Sabbath commandments. By healing on the Sabbath, however, Jesus ran into opposition from some pious fellow-Jews who interpreted the Sabbath laws more narrowly than others did.

Through his preaching and healing, Jesus made the love of God visible, a love which wants to reveal itself in compassion for humankind, and he offered the consolation of forgiveness with it. For Jesus, as for Judaism, the will of God revealed in the Torah was like a mirror, in which people could see who God is and who they themselves are. The human inability to live according to God's will throws a person upon the compassion and love of God, who is ready to grant forgiveness to anyone who earnestly desires it.

Jesus—Prophet and Messiah of Israel

All of this does not yet fully describe the influence and importance of Jesus. As much as Jesus lived as a Jew among his people, within these people he nevertheless occupied a special position. His life and work also had prophetic characteristics. Jesus applied the criticism of the Old Testament prophets to his own people and to a narrow-minded interpretation of the Torah, and he carried the prophetic message further in his own teaching and actions. He granted forgiveness of sins and at the same time announced the coming of God's kingdom. He gathered a circle of 12 disciples (corresponding to the 12 tribes of Israel) around him and called people to discipleship. Above all, he gave his attention to those who were poor, sick, or outcasts from society.

Through all of this, Jesus gained an authority to which his followers responded with the confession that he was the Messiah, the long-awaited Deliverer of Israel. The things Jesus did and said brought him into conflict with others: the political rulers found their own power threatened; the religious authorities did not see their expectations for the Redeemer realized in him. Even his own followers could not understand the way in which Jesus deliberately took suffering on himself.

Jesus' suffering and death on the cross took place in full submission to the will of God. The path of humility which he followed was determined by love for God and for people. Even on the cross, he prayed for his executioners and for those condemned with him. He died with Jewish prayers on his lips (for example, Psalm 22).

According to the New Testament, the resurrection of Jesus led his followers to believe that his death was an event willed by God which had meaning for Israel, and through Israel for the entire world. From this point on, the Jewish followers of Jesus understood Jesus' suffering and death as an act of substitution, which had validity for every one of their people who saw in the "mirror of the Torah" his or her own true condition before the holy God.

Because of these experiences which were brought about by the resurrection event, belief in Jesus as the Christ caught fire among the Jewish people. The title of honor, *Christ* (Messiah), was added to the name *Jesus,* which thus testified and confessed that Jesus of Nazareth was the Messiah. The conviction that the sacrifice of Jesus the Jew was God's offer of salvation, first proclaimed by and for Jews, became an essential truth for the Jewish-Christian community. Soon it was realized that this offer of salvation was also valid for the Gentiles

In addition, it should not be forgotten that Israel gave the Christ to the world ("salvation is from the Jews," John 4:22). In the course of its history Christianity has for the most part forgotten this fact, and only recently have Christians begun to think more intensively about what it means.

The majority of Jews, however, have not understood Jesus to be the Messiah. In recent Judaism, a growing interest in Jesus can be detected, even to the point of an attempt by some scholars to "bring Jesus home to Judaism." This makes it all the more clear that Jesus was not opposed to the Jewish people and their faith. Some Jews are prepared to grant Jesus a place of honor among the righteous and the teachers of Israel.

The paths of Jews and Christians are coming closer together in regard to the person of Jesus. However, this convergence comes to a halt when Christians confess Jesus of Nazareth to be the risen one, the Christ, the Savior, and the Son of God. The Jewish scholar Shalom ben-Chorin put it this way: "The faith of Jesus unites us, faith in Jesus separates us."

19

Passover and the Lord's Supper

The celebration of the Lord's Supper has special significance for the worship life of Christians; in the same way, the celebration of the Passover stands out for Jews as the center of one of the major festivals in the year. A comparison of Passover and the Lord's Supper can point out the things they have in common.

The Origin and History of the Passover Festival

Hints and brief remarks in various Old Testament passages indicate that the festival called the Passover (*Pesach*) has had a long history, during which it has been understood and interpreted in a variety of ways. In the view of both Christian and Jewish scholars, the prehistory of the Passover includes a nomadic shepherd festival, which was celebrated by the extended family in the early part of the year when the pasture land was cultivated. Another early stage in the development of Passover is assumed to have been the Festival of Unleavened Bread (*matzot*), which farmers celebrated in the spring, at the beginning of the barley harvest.

After the exodus from Egypt and Israel's settlement in the land of Canaan, Passover was a festival celebrated by the whole people. As a celebration remembering and reenacting the exodus, it became one of the most important festivals in Israel. The two components in its background are tied together in the common meal at the Passover celebration: from the one side, the slaughter of the Passover lamb and the symbolic action involving the blood of the lamb (Exod. 12:21-24), and from the other, the unleavened bread made from the grain of the new harvest. The various elements of the Passover, such as words, gestures, and foods, represent the saving acts of God, who led the people of God out of Egypt. In this way the Passover festival becomes a visible expression of the faith of Israel.

As a festival of all Israel, the Passover was, during the time of the monarchy, connected with the temple in Jerusalem and celebrated there with the entire family. Following the destruction of the temple and the Babylonian exile, Passover became the main festival of the Jewish family and came to symbolize remembrance and hope. As the Mishnah says:

In every generation a man is bound to regard himself as though he personally had gone forth from Egypt. . . . Therefore it is our duty to thank, praise, laud, glorify, exalt, honor, bless, extol, and adore him who wrought all these miracles for our fathers and ourselves; He brought us forth from bondage into freedom, from sorrow into joy, from mourning into festivity, from darkness into great light, and from servitude into redemption.

(*The Babylonian Talmud: Seder Mo'ed,* Tractate *Pesachim* X, 5, trans. and ed. I. Epstein, Soncino Press, 1938, pp. 595-596).

The Celebration of the Passover Festival

The biblical directions for the Passover festival are found in Exod. 12:1-13,16; Lev. 23:5-8; Num. 28:16-25; and Deut. 16:1-8. The Tractate *Pesachim* in the Mishnah and the Passover Haggadah (in its present form, dating from the 10th century) regulate the course of the Passover and especially the important seder evening which takes place during the festival.

The Passover festival lasts eight days (seven in Israel), with special prominence given to the beginning and the end. Synagogue worship services during Passover are much the same as the usual Sabbath services. During the service the "festival scroll," the Song of Solomon, is read, understood as praise of God's love for God's people. Outside the land of Israel an eighth day was added long ago, in order to make up for uncertainties in the tradition about the beginning of the festival. (For descriptions of Passover customs, see pp. 91-92 and pp. 102-105.)

The Passover is not a sacrament for the Jews. The bread, wine, and other "elements" of the Passover meal are, for Jews, symbols or signs which represent God's saving acts. Food and faith, joy and sorrow, memories and hope are all here tied together in a manner typical of the Jewish faith. The festival binds the earlier generations with those of the present and future and points forward to the coming redemption in the kingdom of God.

The Lord's Supper in the New Testament

The farewell meal which Jesus shared with his disciples on the evening before his crucifixion can only be understood in connection with the Passover, even if it has not been clearly established whether it was a Passover meal in the traditional sense. Just as in the Passover meal, Jesus broke bread and drank wine with his friends, and both actions were accompanied with words of explanation, prayers of thanks, and songs of praise. Just as in the Passover meal, this supper included dialog, responses, and remembrance of God's saving acts and of the instituting of the meal. Jesus spoke of "remembrance" and called for the repetition of the celebration. The eating and the drinking have to do with fellowship with one another and with fellowship with God; the meal also looks toward the coming of the Messiah.

The gospel writers and Paul (in 1 Corinthians 11) took seriously the connection between the Passover and the Lord's Supper. The Christian community has looked to the Passover to understand not only Jesus' Last Supper, but also his death: Jesus himself takes the place of the Passover lamb and participates in its death and in that which this death brings about (John 1:29 and 19:14; 1 Cor. 5:7-8).

Passover and the Lord's Supper

Both Passover and the Lord's Supper are festive meals that have biblical foundations. When Jesus instituted the Lord's Supper, he consciously connected it with Jewish Passover customs and with the beliefs associated with them. Both celebrations have a dialogical character and a fixed liturgical order and yet have gone through historical development, both in form and in meaning. Both celebrations have to do with the memory of a deliverance, with a redemption, and with a reenactment of saving events and fellowship at a meal which is the visible sign for the coming fellowship in the kingdom of God. To this day the bread or wafer used in the Christian celebration of the Lord's Supper is often the *matzot* or unleavened bread of the Passover.

For Jews, Passover means remembering their liberation from suffering and slavery; Christians believe that in the Lord's Supper they receive the benefits of the saving work of Jesus Christ. For Christians, bread and wine as well as the entire celebration fulfill the promise of the presence of the Lord.

In the Lord's Supper, Christians continue to have table fellowship with their Lord, and his death and resurrection are proclaimed. In this way the reference to the freeing and delivering work of Jesus Christ takes the place of the connection which the Passover has with the deliverance from Egypt.

Through this new interpretation of the Passover meal, the festival of God's new covenant with all people has come into being, a festival that is celebrated often, not only in the springtime. The remembrance of God's saving acts continues to bring those acts into the present, and gives hope for traveling the path to perfect freedom, even if the first part of that path still leads through the "wilderness."

Excerpt from the Passover Haggadah

The Passover festival is celebrated as the "time of our liberation" and "in memory of the exodus from Egypt." Part of that festival is the seder evening, which includes the breaking and distributing of three loaves of unleavened bread (*matzot*), accompanied by prayers of thanksgiving, and drinking from four cups of wine during the course of the evening meal.

At the beginning of the seder evening the seder plate with the symbolic foods on it is lifted up, at which time the one leading the celebration says:

This is the bread of poverty which our forefathers ate in the land of Egypt. Let all who are hungry enter and eat; let all who are needy come to our Passover feast. This year we are here; next year may we be in the Land of Israel. This year we are slaves; next year may we be free men.

(*The Passover Haggadah,* Nahum N. Glatzer, Schocken, 1953, p. 21.)

The Words of Institution of the Christian Lord's Supper

In the Christian celebration of the Lord's Supper, the following words are said before the bread and wine are distributed:

. . . the Lord Jesus on the night when he was betrayed took bread, and when he had given thanks, he broke it, and said, "This is my body which is for you. Do this in remembrance of me." In the same way also the cup, after supper, saying, "This cup is the new covenant in my blood. Do this, as often as you drink it, in remembrance of me." For as often as you eat this bread and drink the cup, you proclaim the Lord's death until he comes (1 Cor. 11:23-26).

20

The Trial of Jesus

Many Christians think that the Jews are responsible
for Jesus' death on the cross. Jews deny this emphatically. Can this argument be settled on the basis of the
New Testament? Do the reports of the evangelists give
a comprehensive picture of the trial which led to the
death of Jesus? Do they allow us to make an unam-
biguous judgment about the course of events? What
meaning does the trial of Jesus have for the encounter
between Jews and Christians today?

How Do Jews See the Trial of Jesus?

Because Jews have for centuries been accused of being
"Christ killers," clearing up matters connected with
the trial of Jesus is especially important. Jews see in
this accusation the roots of anti-Semitism among Christians. On the basis of certain passages from the New
Testament (Mark 14:1; John 11:53; Acts 2:36; 3:15;
5:30; 1 Thess. 2:14-15), many Christians have held
the entire Jewish people to be guilty of the death of
Jesus. Using this as a reason, Christians have persecuted Jews in terrible ways, from the Middle Ages
down to our own time. The charge of "Christ killers"
has served as the justification time and time again.

Consequently, Jewish and Christian scholars who
study the New Testament today must carefully examine
the reports about the trial of Jesus in the Gospels for
any clues about who was actually responsible for Jesus'
death. Scholars point out that it was not Jews who

sentenced Jesus to death according to the Roman law and in the Roman manner (that is, by crucifixion), but the Roman governor Pontius Pilate, who had Jesus executed by his soldiers. Along with this, they point to the Apostles' and Nicene Creeds, which clearly testify that Jesus suffered and was crucified "under Pontius Pilate."

In addition, scholars emphasize that Jesus was respected among the Jewish people, and in many matters was especially close to the scribes and the Pharisees. It was not these people, but rather the wealthy and politically motivated high priestly families who took part in capturing Jesus and turning him over to Pilate. Scholars also point to contradictions among the Gospels in the description of the legal proceedings before the Sanhedrin. Finally, they express the suspicion that the Christian tradition wanted to lay all the blame on the Jews and absolve Pilate from his guilt in order to make Christianity acceptable to the Romans and the Greeks.

How Does the New Testament See the Trial of Jesus?

The following conception is widespread in Christianity: The leading Jews wanted to do away with Jesus; the entire high council (the Sanhedrin) sentenced Jesus to death for blasphemy; Pilate was forced into the execution of Jesus by the leading Jews and the Jewish people collectively. Therefore the terrible suffering of the Jews throughout history can be seen as God's punishment for their guilt in the death of Jesus.

This view cannot be supported by the New Testament texts, first of all because the purpose of the New Testament is to proclaim God's will and plan of salvation in the story of Jesus' suffering, and not primarily to provide information about the course of the trial. That is why the Gospels leave open so many questions about exact details, concerning which scholars continue to debate to this day. Here is one example of differing statements in two gospels: Was Jesus sentenced to death by the high council because of blasphemy (Mark 14:64) or was he charged before Pilate as a politically dangerous Messiah, that is, as "King of the Jews" (Luke 22:67—23:2)? Since the only source for the trial of Jesus is the Gospels, the details of the course of the trial cannot be determined with certainty.

The gospel reports indicate that various Jewish groups became opponents of Jesus (see Mark 11 and 12, for example) and raised the suspicion of dangerous political activity with the political rulers (for example, Luke 13:31-32). However, the Gospels do not raise questions about the guilt of people but rather about the intention of God: Couldn't Jesus have avoided a confrontation in Jerusalem, his capture, and his sentence? Why did he have to follow this path? Why did he do so willingly?

The collective New Testament witness answers the questions in this way: Jesus' way of suffering was God's decision and God's will. The meaning of his death is the reconciliation of sinful humanity with God (2 Cor. 5:18-21) and with it the forgiveness of all human guilt (Matt. 26:28). The necessity of his suffering and death is explained in this way long before his capture (Mark 8:31; 9:31; 10:33-34) as well as after his resurrection (Luke 24:26, 46).

Who Is Guilty of Jesus' Death?

The New Testament emphasizes not only the participation of the Jewish leadership in handing Jesus over for crucifixion, but also the responsibility of the Jewish ruler Herod Antipas, who had John the Baptist be-headed, and the Roman governor Pilate, who was known for his cruelty to Jews (Luke 13:1). These rulers realized that Jesus was innocent (Luke 23:14-15) and should have set him free. The New Testament shows that they did not do this, but put political advantage above what was right in making a judgment (Acts 4:27). According to the Gospels, Jesus' disciples also carried special guilt: they did not stay awake with him in Gethsemane and they all deserted him when he was captured; Judas betrayed him; their spokesman, Peter, denied him.

So all parties concerned failed in their responsibility to Jesus: the disciples of Jesus as well as the leaders of Jesus' people, the people themselves, and also the political rulers, both Gentile and Jewish.

Who is guilty of Jesus' death? The testimony of the New Testament says it clearly: *everyone* is guilty. At the trial of Jesus it is evident that all people, then as now, "have sinned and fall short of the glory of God" (Rom. 3:23). Seen in this way, we are all "Christ killers" and cannot lay that charge on individual persons or groups. Many of the passion hymns express this truth:

Who was the guilty? Who brought this upon thee?
Alas, my treason, Jesus, hath undone thee.
'Twas I, Lord Jesus, I it was denied thee;
I crucified thee.

("Ah, Holy Jesus")

The Trial of Jesus and Jews Today

There is no justification for the fact that of all those who participated in bringing about Jesus' death, for centuries, only the Jews have received the blame for what happened. When the New Testament reports are interpreted to suggest that the Jews who did not see Jesus as the Messiah even today still bear a particular responsibility for Jesus' death, this interpretation must be seen as an unjust attack. Even though some Jewish people and groups participated in the trial of Jesus, Jews of today carry no greater guilt for Jesus' death than any other people do. Christians need to correct both their thinking and their behavior accordingly.

The cry of the Jewish crowd before Pilate, "His blood be on us and our children!" (Matt. 27:25) often has been cited to transfer blame to later generations. But this saying, found only in Matthew, has been disastrously misinterpreted. Its meaning in its immediate context applies only to those directly participating at that time; they wanted to persuade Pilate to have Jesus executed, and they wanted to make clear that they—along with their families—were ready to take the responsibility. This passage was first interpreted in the fourth century as a "curse upon themselves for all time," in connection with disputes between Christians and Jews at that time. Even if the passage were understood as a "self-curse," this could by no means compel God to pronounce the speakers and their descendants forever guilty and to punish them forever, especially since the blood of Jesus, according to the New Testament witness, serves precisely as atonement for all people.

We Christians of today should model ourselves after the first Jewish followers of Jesus. Despite their often harsh disputes with Judaism, they held great respect for Israel as the chosen people of God (Rom. 9:3-5) and admonished one another not to be arrogant toward the Jews (Rom. 11:16-24), but to consider them as neighbors and to love them (Mark 12:28-34).

A Statement on Deicide and the Jews

The House of Bishops of the Episcopal Church issued this statement in 1964:

The poison of anti-Semitism has causes of a political, national, psychological, social, and economic nature. It has often sought religious justification in the events springing from the crucifixion of Jesus. Anti-Semitism is a direct contradiction of Christian doctrine. Jesus was a Jew, and, since the Christian Church is rooted in Israel, spiritually we are Semites.

The charge of deicide against the Jews is a tragic misunderstanding of the inner significance of the crucifixion. To be sure, Jesus was crucified by *some* soldiers at the instigation of *some* Jews. But, this cannot be construed as imputing corporate guilt to every Jew in Jesus' day, much less the Jewish people in subsequent generations. Simple justice alone proclaims the charge of a corporate or inherited curse on the Jewish people to be false.

Furthermore, in the dimension of faith the Christian understands that all men are guilty of the death of Christ, for all have in some manner denied Him; and since the sins that crucified Christ were common human sins, the Christian knows that he himself is guilty. But he rejoices in the words and spirit of his Lord who said for the Roman soldiers and for all responsible for His crucifixion, "Father, forgive them, for they know not what they do."

PART SIX

CHRISTIANS
AND JEWS

21

Anti-Semitism

Anti-Semitism is a technically inaccurate term which has nevertheless been widely used to describe anti-Jewish attitudes and propaganda during recent history. The Arabs are also Semitic people, but anti-Semitic slogans or actions have not been directed against them. Since about 1880 it has become customary to apply the term *Semites* in a polemic and mocking manner to the Jews. Out of this practice came the misleading word *anti-Semitism*. It had a scholarly air about it, was tied to a theory about race, and disguised what was really meant: hatred of Jews. How has this hostility toward Jews come about? What part have Christians had in it?

Hostility toward Jews in the 19th and 20th Centuries

After hundreds of years of alternation between periods of limited toleration and times of bloody persecution, the period known as the Enlightenment brought something of an emancipation to the Jews. With new possibilities open to them, Jews tried to enter into areas which had previously been closed to them, especially in art, scholarship, and politics. Anti-Jewish propaganda then arose which accused them of "immorality," "foreign infiltration of the national heritage," and "degeneracy."

During the 19th century, an increasingly stronger sense of nationalism developed throughout Europe, in which the Jews in their respective environments also participated. But since there were Jews in almost every country, it was not long before they were scorned as "internationalists," "homeless," an "untrustworthy race" or even as "inferior." From this it was only a small step to the damning of "Jewish blood" and to racist anti-Semitism, which at that time was still promoted under scholarly trimmings.

Many pioneers of national movements were infected with such ideologies, in countries such as Germany, Hungary, Czechoslovakia, and Poland. Especially bloody pogroms took place in Czarist Russia. (The word *pogrom* comes from the Russian and means "deadly destruction.") In the German empire, hatred of Jews became an object of "scientific" investigations and was therefore socially acceptable. Paul de Lagarde (1827–1891), professor at Göttingen University, distanced himself from a vulgar anti-Semitism, yet called for the cleansing of the "German-Christian religion" from everything Jewish. He said that in *one* nation there could be only *one* soul. Adolf Stoecker (1835-1909), the Kaiser's chaplain, portrayed the Jews as "without any creative power in religion" and as "chasing after the false gods of gold." Large circles within liberal Protestantism and also within the clergy of Catholicism were of an anti-Semitic mind.

Hitler was able to make use of this anti-Semitism inherited from the 19th century as a unifying bond for his efforts at national renewal. So German National Socialism (nazism) in its earliest beginnings was linked up with explicit hostility against Jews. The weekly paper *Der Stürmer* (The Assailant), published by ardent Nazi Julius Streicher, was especially aimed at inciting hatred of Jews. By means of *Der Stürmer,* slogans like *"Die Juden sind unser Unglück"* (The

Jews are our misfortune) or *"Deutschland erwache— Juda verrecke"* (Germany awake—Jews die) were hammered into the minds of the public.

The progressive development from the pseudoacademic forms of anti-Semitism to the mass murder of millions of Jews calls for some fundamental thinking about the origin of this ideology

The Christian West and the Jews

After the decay of the Roman Empire in the West, the situation of Jews in the Christian territories which emerged was at first very diverse. In the western Gothic empire around Spain, Jews were severely oppressed, while in the Frankish empire Jewish life developed richly, from the Rhine to Prague. The time of the Crusades brought an end to this tolerance: in 1096 thousands of Jews were killed in pogroms; entire communities were wiped out. This persecution of Jews arose from the conviction that the "enemies of the cross" had to be overcome not only in Palestine, but also in their own countries. Later on, rabbis in many places were forced to take part in disputations that were supposed to show the superiority of the teachings of Christianity. The Fourth Lateran Council of 1215 decreed that Jews had to wear special clothing which set them apart from the Christian population.

Forced into isolation in this manner, the Jews were branded as scapegoats in a variety of ways. They were slandered as murderers of small children, as violators of the bread consecrated for the Lord's Supper, and as poisoners of wells. When a plague devastated Europe in 1348, it was portrayed as God's punishment on Christianity for not removing the Jews from their midst. All of this led to the destruction of many Jewish communities and the expulsion of Jews from still other communities in Central Europe. Most Jews fled to Eastern Europe, holding onto their Jewish-German dialect, Yiddish, as their everyday language; some of these later returned to countries in Western Europe. Similarly, the Jews of the Iberian peninsula—after it had been won back for Christianity in 1492—were forced either to be baptized or to leave the country.

Humanism and the Reformation were at first friendly toward the Jews; Martin Luther also expressed a positive attitude toward them at first. The newly awakened interest in the Hebrew language and in the Old Testament had a favorable effect on Christian relationships to the Jews. But the unity of the state and the church remained a fundamental principle in the emerging Protestant states, just as it had been in the Middle Ages. Full rights of citizenship were inconceivable for those who were of a different religion, and hostility toward Jews began anew.

Martin Luther was disappointed in his hopes that the Jews would be won over for Christianity. They appeared to him as a people who willfully disdained the love of God. In 1543 Luther went so far as to demand that the synagogues be burned down, Jewish homes be destroyed, the books of the Talmud be confiscated, the rabbis be prohibited from teaching, and the lives of Jews be made difficult in still other ways. Since that time, enemies of Jews have time and again called on Luther for support.

Luther's shocking demands and the events leading up to them compel us to ask about the roots of hatred for Jews among Christians.

Hostility toward Jews in the New Testament?

An essential root of hostility toward Jews among Christians is the so-called anti-Semitism in the New Testament. Here a distinction needs to be made between earlier and later writings and between statements and their later interpretation.

The dispute between Jesus and some of the leaders of Judaism can still be considered an inner-Jewish conflict. Paul did not keep restating the sharp accusations he made in 1 Thess. 2:14-16, which were evoked by the situation he was addressing. In Romans 9–11 he pursued the question of the history of salvation, asking why God had allowed Israel to turn away from Jesus. In these chapters Paul testified to his ultimate hope for Israel (see p. 205). There remained, however, an insoluable contradiction. Paul said that because the Jews had rejected the gospel, they were "enemies of God, for your sake," but because God had chosen them, they were God's beloved (Rom. 11:28).

The later writings of the New Testament are partially influenced by the historical experience of the growing alienation of Christians from Judaism. In producing the accounts of the suffering and death of Jesus, the Christian community allowed Pilate's responsibility to recede and emphasized the responsibility of the Jewish leadership. This tendency comes to its sharpest expression in John 8:44, where "the Jews" are told: "You are of your father the devil." Alongside this, however, is also found the statement in John 4:22: ". . . salvation is from the Jews."

Hostility toward Jews as a form of hatred of strangers had existed for a long time in the ancient world. This also had an effect on the early Christian

185

church, and has also contributed to the fact that statements in the New Testament down through history have been increasingly interpreted in a way which is hostile to Jews.

Anti-Semitism: An Error Which Has Been Corrected?

Christians must realize that anti-Semitism is a form of unrepentance. If Christians do not fully recognize God's choosing of Israel, the roots of their own Christian existence are affected. Therefore, Christians are obliged by their own faith to oppose anti-Semitism in any form and to make it possible for Jews to live according to their faith, in freedom and dignity.

One thing further should be said: both Christians and Jews have the right to disagree with the policies of the State of Israel without being accused of anti-Semitism.

Christian Anti-Judaism in the Middle Ages

The woodcut, "The Jewish Mirror," reprinted on p. 187, was probably also used as a pamphlet, and illustrates the anti-Judaism of the Middle Ages. Baptism is portrayed as the work of the holy and believing church, while Jewish circumcision appears as the work of the devil.

Martin Luther's Anti-Judaism

Luther's treatise of 1543, *On the Jews and Their Lies,* has caused dismay among the reformer's friends and followers ever since it first appeared. It was not made available in English until 1971. The translator prefaces the work with these words:

Both editor and publisher, therefore, wish to make clear at the very outset that the publication of this treatise is being

Der Joeden spiegel.

An anti-Jewish cartoon from the Middle Ages depicts Baptism as the faithful action of the church and circumcision as the work of the devil.

undertaken only to make available the necessary documents for scholarly study of this aspect of Luther's thought, which has played so fateful a role in the development of anti-Semitism in Western culture. Such publication is in no way intended as an endorsement of the distorted views of Jewish faith and practice or the defamation of the Jewish people which this treatise contains. . . . It is hoped that the publication of the present treatise, unpleasant as its contents are, will contribute to greater candor concerning the role which Christians have played in this dark story. As Aarne Siirala has written, "The way in which the often suppressed facts of the history of the persecution and discrimination against the Jews are brought into the consciousness of Christians will be one decisive element in our being a church of repentance and faith in our generation."

(*Luther's Works* 47, Fortress, 1971, pp. 123, 133-134.)

The year 1983 was the 500th anniversary of Luther's birth. The theme of the Second Consultation between Representatives of The International Jewish Committee for Interreligious Consultation and The Lutheran World Federation, held in Stockholm in July 1983, was "Luther, Lutheranism, and the Jews." Among the statements resulting from this consultation were the following:

Statement by Lutheran participants

We Lutherans take our name and much of our understanding of Christianity from Martin Luther. But we cannot accept or condone the violent verbal attacks that the Reformer made against the Jews. . . .

The sins of Luther's anti-Jewish remarks, the violence of his attacks on the Jews, must be acknowledged with deep distress. And all occasions for similar sin in the present or the future must be removed from our churches . . . .

Lutherans of today refuse to be bound by all of Luther's utterances on the Jews. We hope we have learned from the tragedies of the recent past. We are responsible for seeing that we do not now or in the future leave any doubt about our position on racial and religious prejudice and that we afford to all the human dignity, freedom and friendship that are the right of all the Father's children.

Statement by the Jewish participants

. . . the Jewish participants welcome the commitment of the Lutheran partners in dialogue to respect the living reality of Judaism from the perspective of Jewish self-understanding and their undertaking that Lutheran writings will never again serve as a source for the teaching of hatred for Judaism and the denigration of the Jewish people. This heralds a new chapter in the relationship between Jews and Lutherans which should find practical expression in teaching, preaching and worship as well as joint activities for social justice, human rights and the cause of peace.

We pledge ourselves to collaborate with our Lutheran colleagues in facing these common challenges. We trust that this year of Martin Luther observances will thus prove a turning point leading to a constructive future between Lutherans and Jews throughout the world.

(*Luther, Lutheranism, and the Jews,* pp. 9-11.)

A Resolution on Anti-Semitism

The following resolution was adopted at the North Carolina State Baptist Convention in 1971. A similar resolution was passed by the Southern Baptist Convention in 1972.

Whereas, anti-Semitism has been a serious problem for the Church through most of the Christian history, and

Whereas, this unchristian attitude on the part of many people led to brutal persecution of the Jews in numerous countries and societies, and

Whereas, the most flagrant and cruel expression of this spiritual malignancy, the Nazi holocaust, transpired in our generation, and

Whereas, latent anti-Semitism lies barely under the surface in many Western, Christian cultures today, and

Whereas, many Christian communions and denominations, including our own, have failed to take a sufficiently vigorous stand against anti-Semitism, and

Whereas, it is clearly a moral and ethical question of the greatest magnitude, and

Whereas, Baptists share with Jews a heritage of persecution and suffering for conscience's sake,

Therefore, be it *Resolved* that this Convention go on record as opposed to any and all forms of anti-Semitism; that it declare anti-Semitism unchristian; that we messengers to this Convention pledge ourselves to combat anti-Semitism in every honorable, Christian way.

Be it further *Resolved* that Southern Baptists covenant to work positively to replace all anti-Semitic bias with the Christian attitude and practice of love for Jews who, along with other men, are equally beloved of God.

22

The Holocaust: Mass Murder of the Jews

For a long time there was no satisfactory term for the mass murder of the Jews by the Germans under Hitler. "The Final Solution," the code word used by the Nazis, is intolerably harmless; "Auschwitz," the name of the most well-known extermination camp, leads to the false assumption that exterminations took place only there. The television series "Holocaust" popularized a term which was first used in English-speaking countries and is now used universally. The term was originally used in connection with sacrifices in the Old Testament, designating the whole burnt offering (see Lev. 3:1). Now it expresses the intent of total extermination by massacre, which was the aim of the highly organized program of mass murder carried out by the Nazis.

The attempt to portray in a television series these events which are beyond all imagination raised anew the questions which have demanded an answer since 1945: What really happened? What is the meaning of the Holocaust for Jews and for Christians?

What Happened?

Hostility against Judaism was a part of National Socialism (nazism) in Germany from the beginning, as the 1920 party platform shows throughout. On the basis of earlier racial theories, every person of Jewish origin—without regard to that person's personal conduct, religion, age, or position in society—was seen as an enemy of the German people. This included Jews who had converted to Christianity, or whose parents had converted.

After the Nazis came to power in 1933, these ideas were quickly translated into actions. By means of numerous laws and ordinances, persons of Jewish origin were more and more clearly singled out from society and isolated. By 1938 the time was ripe for the first large-scale action against Jews throughout Germany, the *Kristallnacht* (night of broken glass), as it was called. On the night of November 9th, 275 synagogues were destroyed and 26,000 people were taken into concentration camps, primarily in Buchenwald and Dachau. After the beginning of World War II, in an effort to isolate Jews even further, they were required to wear the "yellow star" as an easily visible badge.

Based on experience gained in the campaign for the elimination of all "unworthy lives" among the German people (the systematic killing of mentally and physically handicapped persons), the organized mass murder of the Jews began in 1941. To carry this out, special extermination camps were set up far to the east (at Chelmno, Belzec, Sobibor, Treblinka, Maidanek, and Auschwitz-Birkenau), in which mass killing with gas was gradually perfected. Persons of Jewish ancestry from the entire sphere of influence of the "Third Reich" were little by little deported to these death camps (which were different from concentration camps)—that is, if they had not already fallen victim to the firing squads of the German SS groups in the occupied areas of Russia.

Completely accurate figures on the number of Jews murdered in the Holocaust are not available. However, on the basis of a variety of increasingly precise calculations (the Nuremberg trials were one important source of information), it has been firmly established that some six million Jewish people became victims of this and other extermination programs. When one considers all those who would have been born from these six million, the horror becomes all the greater.

What Does the Holocaust Mean for Jews?

Two-thirds of the Jews in Europe, more than a third of all Jews living at that time, died in the Holocaust. This fact indicates how directly the Holocaust was and is experienced by the Jews as a deadly threat. No other event in the long history of Jewish persecution so directly threatened the physical existence of Judaism. From this point on, a new era of Jewish history began.

Those suffering the consequences of the Holocaust are not only the survivors of the death camps, who carry the tatooed camp number with them for a lifetime. Hardly any Jews living today whose families came from Europe do not have close relatives among the victims.

Out of the shock over the experience of the Holocaust arose a deep searching and questioning among Jews in all parts of the world: How can a Jew live among people who were capable of this kind of cold-blooded, merciless hatred? How is one to understand the guidance of God in such an event?

But out of this shock the Jewish hope for a state of their own also gained enormous impetus. With the courage of those who are desperate, the Jews fought to establish a land in which they would no longer be a threatened minority. The will to survive, unyielding determination to defend themselves against any attack, and uncompromising toughness have become the characteristics of the young State of Israel since its birth.

What Does the Holocaust Mean for Christians?

In Germany during the Nazi period it was dangerous to show concern about the fate of the Jews or to help them in any way. Even the churches remained mostly silent. Only a small number of individuals disobeyed and helped Jews, at the risk of their own lives. The great majority kept to themselves, did not want to know too much, but approved in principle of "strict action" against Jews. For these reasons a relatively small number of active accomplices of Hitler were able to carry out his extermination plan with little interference.

How can one still praise the God "who over all things so wondrously reigneth" after the Holocaust? This has become a serious question for many believing Christians. Many far too innocent conceptions of the reality of God have vanished in the face of the Holocaust; the traditional picture of God has been called into question. A deeper understanding of what Christ's suffering means for the faith has emerged.

But the traditional picture of humankind has also been called into question. The idea of a gradual development of humankind to an increasingly pure form of humanity has been shattered. In the Holocaust, human capabilities for evil came to light which had long been considered overcome. A new insight into the powerful reality of evil has been given.

The shocking realization that what happened took place in "Christian" lands—with the consent of Christians and Christian churches, or at least without their sufficiently energetic opposition—has given rise to an intensive questioning and searching, leading directly to a theology of the Holocaust in the United States. Here the Holocaust is understood as a fundamental issue for all theology and for the church. It necessitates new and thorough thinking in all areas, above all in regard to the relationship between Christians and Jews.

Lessons from the Holocaust

The mass murder of the Jews is most often thought about only as a problem of the past that will recede further and further into the distance as time goes on. But the question must be emphatically directed to the present and the future: How can we make sure that an event like the Holocaust never again occurs, now or in the future? How can we educate young people so that they are alert to all attempts to exploit their talents for inhuman purposes? How can we overcome prejudices against individuals and entire groups of people? How can we authentically bear witness to the love of God for all people?

The Holocaust issues a challenge to all people, especially to Christians and Jews. It is a warning, which cannot be ignored, to put a stop to all inhuman acts as soon as they begin.

"Chorus of the Rescued" by Nelly Sachs

The Jewish poet Nelly Sachs, who received the Nobel Prize in 1975, wrote this in 1946:

We, the rescued,
From whose hollow bones death had begun to whittle
    his flutes,

And on whose sinews he had already stroked his bow—
Our bodies continue to lament
With their mutilated music.
We, the rescued,
The nooses wound for our necks still dangle
before us in the blue air—
Hourglasses still fill with our dripping blood.
We, the rescued,
The worms of fear still feed on us.
Our constellation is buried in dust.
We, the rescued,
Beg you:
Show us your sun, but gradually.
Lead us from star to star, step by step.
Be gentle when you teach us to live again.
Lest the song of a bird,
Or a pail being filled at the well,
Let our badly sealed pain burst forth again
and carry us away—
We beg you:
Do not show us an angry dog, not yet—
It could be, it could be
That we will dissolve into dust—
Dissolve into dust before your eyes.
For what binds our fabric together?
We whose breath vacated us,
Whose soul fled to him out of that midnight
Long before our bodies were rescued
Into the ark of the moment.
We, the rescued,
We press your hand
We look into your eye—
But all that binds us together now is leave-taking,
The leave-taking in the dust
Binds us together with you.

(Nelly Sachs, *O, The Chimneys,* Farrar, Straus and Giroux, 1967.)

Excerpt from Action by Evangelical Church of the Rhineland, Germany

In January 1980, the regular Synod of the Protestant Church in the Rhineland approved a statement entitled, "Toward Renovation of the Relationship of Christians and Jews." The statement included the following paragraphs:

(1) Stricken, we confess the co-responsibility and guilt of German Christendom for the Holocaust.

(2) We confess thankfully the "Scriptures" of the Jewish people (Luke 24:27; 1 Cor. 15:3f.), our Old Testament, to be the common foundation for the faith and work of Jews and Christians.

(3) We confess Jesus Christ the Jew, who as the Messiah of the Jews is the Savior of the world and binds the peoples of the world to the people of God.

(4) We believe in the permanent election of the Jewish people as the people of God and realize that through Jesus Christ the church is taken into the covenant of God with His people.

(5) We believe with the Jews that the unity of righteousness and love characterizes the saving work of God in history. We believe with the Jews that righteousness and love are the admonitions of God for our whole life. As Christians we see both rooted and grounded in the work of God with the Jewish people and in the work of God through Jesus Christ.

(6) We believe that in their calling Jews and Christians are always witnesses of God in the presence of the world and before each other. Therefore, we are convinced that the

church may not express its witness toward the Jewish people as it does its mission to the peoples of the world.

(7) Therefore, we declare:

Throughout centuries the word "new" has been used against the Jewish people in biblical exegesis: the new covenant was understood as contrast to the old covenant, the new people of God as replacement of the old people of God. This obliviousness to the permanent election of the Jewish people and its relegation to non-existence marked Christian theology, church preaching and church work ever and again right to the present day. Thereby we have also made ourselves guilty of the physical elimination of the Jewish people.

Therefore, we want to perceive the unbreakable connection of the New Testament with the Old Testament in a new way, and learn to understand the relationship of the "old" and "new" from the standpoint of the promise: as a result of the promise, as fulfillment of the promise, as confirmation of the promise. "New" means therefore no replacement of the "old." Hence we deny that the people Israel has been rejected by God or that it has been superseded by the church.

(8) As we are turning around we begin to discover what Christians and Jews both give witness to:

We both confess God as the creator of heaven and earth, and know that we are singled out in the ordinary life of the world by the same God by means of the blessing of Aaron.

We confess the common hope in a new heaven and a new earth and the power of this messianic hope for the witness and work of Christians and Jews for justice and peace in the world.

Excerpt from Night by Elie Wiesel

Elie Wiesel won the Nobel Peace Prize in 1986. In the spring of 1944, at the age of 15, he was deported with his family to Auschwitz and then Buchenwald concentration camps. His book *Night* is an unforgettable telling of that story:

Never shall I forget that night, the first night in camp, which has turned my life into one long night, seven times cursed and seven times sealed. Never shall I forget that smoke. Never shall I forget the little faces of the children, whose bodies I saw turned into wreaths of smoke beneath a silent blue sky.

Never shall I forget those flames which consumed my faith forever.

Never shall I forget that nocturnal silence which deprived me, for all eternity, of the desire to live. Never shall I forget those moments which murdered my God and my soul and turned my dreams to dust. Never shall I forget those things, even if I am condemned to live as long as God Himself. Never. . . .

One day when we came back from work, we saw three gallows rearing up in the assembly place, three black crows. Roll call. SS all around us, machine guns trained: the traditional ceremony. Three victims in chains—and one of them, the little servant, the sad-eyed angel.

The SS seemed more preoccupied, more disturbed than usual. To hang a young boy in front of thousands of spectators was no light matter. The head of the camp read the verdict. All eyes were on the child. He was lividly pale, almost calm, biting his lips. The gallows threw its shadow over him. . . .

The three victims mounted together onto the chairs.

The three necks were placed at the same moment within the nooses.

"Long live liberty!" cried the two adults.

But the child was silent.

"Where is God? Where is He?" someone behind me asked.

At a sign from the head of the camp, the three chairs tipped over.

Total silence throughout the camp. On the horizon, the sun was setting.

"Bare your heads!" yelled the head of the camp. His voice was raucous. We were weeping.

"Cover your heads!"

Then the march past began. The two adults were no longer alive. Their tongues hung swollen, blue-tinged. But the third rope was still moving, being so light, the child was still alive. . . .

For more than half an hour he stayed there, struggling between life and death, dying in slow agony under our eyes. And we had to look him full in the face. He was still alive when I passed in front of him. His tongue was still red, his eyes not yet glazed.

Behind me, I heard the same man asking:

"Where is God now?"

And I heard a voice within me answer him:

"Where is He? Here He is—He is hanging here on this gallows. . . ."

(Elie Wiesel, *Night,* Hill and Wang, 1969, pp. 44, 75-76.

23

Jewish Hope
and Christian Hope

Human beings cannot live without hope. In our culture, hope means to move toward a goal and to have a future. Few people know that this understanding of hope has its origin in the Old Testament, which is common to Jews and Christians. In the Old Testament, to hope means to be wholly oriented toward God, who is leading the world God has created to its fulfillment.

Is this hope still common among Jews today? To what degree does Christian hope include the Jews and the State of Israel?

Hope in the Old Testament

The Old Testament testifies that God calls human beings, joins them together into his people, and leads them to a goal; the goal is hidden, but with trust in God and God's promises they can move toward it.

The story begins with Abraham. God called him out of his homeland to go to an unknown land and gave him a promise which pointed to the distant future: "In you all the families of the earth shall be blessed" (Gen. 12:1-3).

Promises such as these were again and again confirmed and renewed in the history of God's people. Under Moses, the people were set free from bondage in Egypt and were led through the wilderness to the promised land. The life of the people flourished in the land of Israel; they gained power and respect in the time of David and the kings after him. But even when the kingdom broke up and when it was destroyed, the Jews experienced the faithfulness of God, who did not abandon them after this catastrophe and who did not take back any promises. After the exile, God gave the Jews a new beginning in their land.

In the high points of their history as well as in the painful times of testing, hope has been rekindled time and again. In the light of the preaching of the prophets, all of these experiences are understood as the guiding of God. In this way Israel's perspective was continually broadened and was extended to the whole of history and the entire world. Hope for the completion of salvation in the last days emerged more and more clearly (see Isa. 49:6). Salvation was awaited, as a time of peace under the rule of the Messiah (Isa. 11:1-9).

Hope in the New Testament

The New Testament testifies that the awaited Deliverer, the Messiah has come in Jesus of Nazareth and with this coming the age of salvation has begun. He has received the name *Christ,* that is, "Messiah" (the anointed). Jesus Christ has been crucified for the sins of the world and God has raised him from the dead; he will come again for judgment. Salvation is to be found in no one else (Acts 4:12). Whoever believes in him will have life which extends beyond death (John 11:25-26).

The Christian community confesses Jesus Christ as the Son of God, the Creator of heaven and earth. All powers must subject themselves to Christ—now invisible, but one day to be revealed; at the time of the end, Jesus will give his kingdom over to the Father (1 Cor. 15:24, 28). The hope in which Christians live will then be fulfilled (1 Cor. 13:12-13). Regarding this, Paul wrote: "For all the promises of God find their Yes in him. That is why we utter the Amen through him, to the glory of God" (2 Cor. 1:20).

Founded on these promises, the church was formed of Jews and Gentiles (Eph. 2:11-22). Christians live at the beginning of the time of salvation, in the tension between the new that they already experience as a gift, and the completion, which is still to come. They await the completion of all things in the return of their Lord in the last days.

Jewish Hope Today

The hope that Jews have is also directed to God's salvation, but it is not tied up with the person of Jesus Christ. Their hope is based on the promises that God made to his people in the Old Testament. Like the psalmists, they wait for the Lord (Pss. 25:3; 39:7). In the contemporary Jewish Prayerbook this hope is expressed as follows: "Strangers say: There is nothing to look forward to, nothing to hope for—Oh be gracious to your people, who hope in your name!" (from the morning prayer); "And so we hope in You, Lord our God, soon to see Your splendor, sweeping idolatry away so that false gods will be utterly destroyed, perfecting earth by Your kingship so that all mankind will invoke Your name, bringing all the earth's wicked back to You, repentant. Then all who live will know that to You every knee must bend, every tongue pledge loyalty" (the *Aleinu* prayer; the title is the first word of the prayer in Hebrew; from *Siddur Sim Shalom: A Prayerbook for Shabbat, Festivals, and Weekdays,* p. 225).

Jewish faith leaves open the details of how this hope is to be realized. Thus Jews are usually cautious in interpreting the biblical promises for the future. Jewish messianic expectation is tied to a future figure. The *Amidah* prayer, expresses this: "Bring to flower the shoot of your servant David. Hasten the advent of Messianic redemption. Each and every day we hope for Your deliverance" (from *Siddur Sim Shalom: A Prayerbook for Shabbat, Festivals, and Weekdays,* p. 115; see pp. 86-89 of this book for the complete prayer). But this expectation is also completely tied up with the destiny of the Jewish people as a whole, with the land which has been regained, with the rebuilding of Jerusalem and the temple, and with a kingdom of peace for all peoples. In all this they are confident that God's faithfulness will be demonstrated over and over. They also expect that God's faithfulness embraces more than this life. They know the hope for the resurrection of the dead. The 13th and final article in the creed of Maimonides, which has become a part of the Prayerbook, says: "I believe that the dead will be resurrected."

Christian Hope for the People of Israel

After the time of Jesus, the Jewish people went their own way. Because of this, Christians have often drawn the conclusion that the Jewish people have forfeited their chosenness. Christians have sometimes said that the role of people of God, together with all the associated promises, has now been wholly taken over by Christianity. According to this view, the Jewish people still have a right to exist as a nation. But their adherence to their own religion, specifically to a messianic hope which is not directed toward Jesus, is interpreted as backwardness and stubbornness.

The new Jewish awareness among Christians, which began during and after the Holocaust, has led to a complete rethinking of the relationship between Christians and Jews from the ground up. After the Holocaust, many traditional ideas have proved to be arrogant and self-righteous. There is a new awareness that God has never revoked his faithfulness to the Jewish people. Chapters 9–11 of the apostle Paul's Letter to the Romans have become especially significant in this connection. In them Paul expressed his hope, based in God, that all Israel will be saved (Rom. 11:26), although in his time he was experiencing a split between Jews who believed in Jesus as the Messiah and other Jews, as well as the addition of people from the non-Jewish world. With this he confirmed what Jesus had announced to the people of Israel: "For I tell you, you will not see me again, until you say, 'Blessed is he who comes in the name of the Lord' " (Matt. 23:39). A community out of Israel will be present when people from all nations praise and worship Jesus as their Lord.

Thus the Jewish people also have a place in the Christian hope for the future. Christians are moving toward the fulfillment of the promise, the beginning of which Paul already saw in those of his people who were acknowledging Jesus as God's Messiah. God stands by God's promises. But the time when the fulfillment and the completion will take place is known only to God; the manner in which God will bring it about is hidden from us. Therefore human calculations and speculations—including those which have to do with the State of Israel—have time and again proved to be in error. God expects our trust. We can count on God to keep God's Word and therefore we can also include Israel in Christian witness and in the hope to which Jesus Christ has called us.

24

Christian Witness among Jews

For most Christians it is self-evident that Christianity ought to spread over the entire earth: "You shall be my witnesses in Jerusalem and in all Judea and Samaria and to the end of the earth" (Acts 1:8); "Always be prepared to make a defense to any one who calls you to account for the hope that is in you" (1 Peter 3:15).

To most Jews, missionary efforts—especially if they also include Jews—are offensive, even disgraceful. In Israel in December 1977, a law was passed to prohibit under penalty of law anyone from leading others to change their religion.

How did Jews come to have this attitude? How should Christian witness among Jews take place today?

Christians and Jews in History

Jesus, his disciples, and the earliest community in Jerusalem preached to their fellow Jews. In the confession "Jesus of Nazareth is the Messiah of Israel," Jews who believed in Jesus as Messiah came together as a movement within their own people.

It was not long, however, before non-Jews were also attracted to the gospel of Jesus Christ. They were accepted into the Christian community without having to make a formal conversion to Judaism at the same time. So in the first generation, the church already consisted of Jews and Gentiles (Eph. 2:11-22; Gal. 3:28).

This division was a hint of what was to come: Christians and Jews would go their own ways, separated from one another by disagreement. At the end of the first century, membership in both church and synagogue at the same time (which until then had been common) was made impossible. The changing legal situation in the Roman Empire made the gap between the two even wider: the Jewish faith was tolerated by the state, while Christianity, understood as being opposed to the state, was persecuted. But with the period that began with Emperor Constantine the Great, the situation changed drastically. Christianity became a state religion that gradually incorporated the entire population; Judaism was the only religion tolerated alongside it. However, the further spread of Judaism was prohibited under penalty of death, and Jews were increasingly exposed to attempts to utilize the power of the state to force them to convert to Christianity.

Then in the Middle Ages, Christian society tolerated the existence of Jews in their midst only with difficulty. The Jews were slandered as "enemies of humanity." In bloody persecutions they were often given only a choice between Baptism or death. Their resistance caused them to appear as enigmatic, impenitent, and stubborn. On the other hand, Jews saw Christians as fundamentally hostile, arbitrary, and hypocritical.

At the time of the Reformation, Martin Luther at first set out on a new path. He wanted to love the Jews as the people of Jesus and to win them for the gospel. When his hopes were frustrated, he gave vent to that frustration with hostile attacks. Not until the Pietistic movement of the 17th and 18th centuries was there a change. Witnesses to the Christian faith went out from Halle, Germany and traveled through Central and Eastern Europe. They renounced any kind of pressure tactics. In their conversations they gained deep respect for the way in which the Jews were faithful to their religion. And on the other side, the Jews recognized the genuine concern and love which these Christians had for the Jewish people. In the 19th century, as the Jews gradually gained equal legal rights with other citizens, the pressure of their Christian environment led many of them to become fully assimilated, even in religious matters. In many professions, being baptized was a condition for promotion.

Along with this, the 19th century saw the beginning of the organized Christian mission to the entire world. Societies for mission to the Jews were formed in England and cities such as Berlin and Basel. In Germany, the Evangelical Lutheran Central Society for Mission to Israel was founded in 1871 at the instigation of the respected biblical scholar and recognized expert on Judaism, Franz Delitzsch. This society understood itself as something of a reform movement. In contrast to many other societies, it expressly renounced any kind of "proselytizing" with the help of state or economic pressures and refused to deal in "success statistics." The society worked for a "truthful knowledge of Judaism among Christians and of Christianity among Jews" through the Institutum Judaicum Delitzschianum, founded in 1886. Delitzsch translated the New Testament into Hebrew, which gave Jews the opportunity to become acquainted with the message about Jesus Christ in the language of their own worship.

The Jewish Mission Called into Question

The modern mission to the Jews has run into a good deal of opposition, above all from anti-Semites. According to this view, anyone who wants to have anything to do with Jews is under suspicion, all the more if that person attempts to bring about understanding of the people and their faith and speaks about a bond between Jews and Christians based on their origins. It was no accident that very early in the Nazi period in Germany, all mission efforts toward Jews were prohibited.

In the Jewish view, missions to the Jews appear as one of the many efforts which Christians have directed against them, designed to estrange them from their faith and to make them into apostates from Judaism. In view of the bitter experiences of persecution and oppression, conversion is looked upon as a question of character and of loyalty; Christians are suspected of using unfair methods in their witness to Jews.

After the Holocaust, people began to realize how much the centuries of injustices on the part of Christians had contributed to that catastrophe. Thus the Jewish mission was called into question by Christians themselves. The Evangelical Kirchentag, a biennial gathering of German Protestants, declared in 1961 that after all that had happened, Christians—at least in Germany—had no right to engage in mission toward the Jews, not then and not in the future. An even more fundamental conclusion of the Kirchentag was that since the Jews are God's people, they do not need the message about Jesus Christ.

Christian Witness among Jews Today

It is true that since 1945, Christians have every reason to engage in a radical rethinking of their relationship to Jews and to avoid every kind of arrogance. For example, the United Evangelical Lutheran Church of Germany formally declared in 1976 that "as living communities of faith, Jews and Christians confess faith in the one God and are responsible for witnessing for that God to the world." Further, "all attempts at conversion" are to be given up "which seek to force a change upon people, including offering them material advantages."

It is a fact, however, that today, as at the time of Jesus, there are people of Jewish origin who confess Jesus as the Messiah of Israel and of their lives. To be sure, they are viewed by Jews as "apostates," estranged from Judaism, and are no longer counted as members of the Jewish community. They may have come upon their confession of Christian faith in completely different ways: as a result of reading the Bible, especially the New Testament, through encounters with Christians, or in other ways. They say, with the apostles: "We cannot but speak of what we have seen and heard" (Acts 4:20). Their total number is small. Many times they are individuals and many times they form groups, celebrate worship, gather in their homes for Bible reading and prayer, and so give witness to their faith in their own surroundings. Many of them emphasize that they do not want to separate themselves from their Jewish people by their faith in Jesus Christ. Christians who live in minority situations will have an appreciation for their special situation, will hear their witness, and will stand at their side.

Today more and more meetings between Christians and Jews are taking place. These meetings should proceed in a spirit of respect for the religious convictions of the other and in readiness to listen to the other's experiences. In this way, useful conversations come about which lead to new understanding and growing trust. It is important that in encounters such as these, that which is central to the faith for both Jews and Christians is not left out. For Christians, this means their faith in Jesus, the Christ. How else could such a meeting be honest? However, such a witness to one's faith should not be considered "proselytizing."

In their encounter with Jews, Christians can learn that mission does not mean the conversion of another through one's own efforts. Christian witness can prove itself to be genuine only through God's Spirit, just as surely as God himself is the Lord of the community that confesses God as the one who gathers the people of God from all peoples.

United Methodist Guidelines for Dialogue between Jews and Christians

The General Conference of The United Methodist Church issued the following guidelines in a statement on Interreligious Dialogue between Jews and Christians in 1972.

a) Wherever possible, conversations with members of Jewish communities should be initiated and maintained through an existing or an ad hoc ecumenical framework. The ecumenical body could begin by accepting the principles in this United Methodist statement as a foundation for the dialogue, or by drafting its own.

b) In the absence of cooperative Christian efforts to explore mutual understanding, tensions, and difficulties, United Methodist initiative (or response to Jewish initiative) is to be encouraged.

c) Christian participants should make clear that they do not justify past injustice done by Christians to Jews and that

211

there is no tenable biblical or theological base for anti-Semitism, and that they themselves wish to be free of it.

d) Joint planning of conversations should emphasize the broad purposes of dialogues and lessen suspicion that conversion is a deliberate intention.

e) Honest differences should be expected and probed seriously, even as areas of agreement and mutual support are discovered.

f) A series of meetings with some guarantee of continuity of participants is necessary for fruitful conversation. False hopes and superficial optimism resulting from a single session together can lead to despair and further alienation.

g) The joint study of that part of our tradition which both groups have in common, the Jewish Bible or the Christian Old Testament, can be of paramount importance. It is here that the foundation of Jewish and Christian existence coincide. A joint study has potential for new insight into our mutual relationship and our togetherness.

h) Conversations which begin exploration of scriptural and traditional heritages may move to political, sociological, and economic investigations and might well result in common action in the causes of human rights.

i) The dialogues should not overlook the rich opportunities afforded in visitation of synagogues and churches and in common prayer and other interreligious services. . . .

World Council of Churches Statement on Authentic Christian Witness

In 1982 the Executive Committee of the World Council of Churches received and commended to the churches for study and action a statement on ''Ecumenical Considerations on Jewish-Christian Dialogue'' (see p. 235

for the full text). The statement included these paragraphs on authentic Christian witness:

4.1 Christians are called to witness to their faith in word and deed. The Church has a mission and it cannot be otherwise. This mission is not one of choice.

4.2 Christians have often distorted their witness by coercive proselytism—conscious and unconscious, overt and subtle. Referring to proselytism between Christian churches, the Joint Working Group of the Roman Catholic Church and the World Council of Churches stated: "Proselytism embraces whatever violates the right of the human person, Christian or non-Christian, to be free from external coercion in religious matters" (*Ecumenical Review,* 1/1971, p. 11).

4.3 Such rejection of proselytism, and such advocacy of respect for the integrity and the identity of all persons and all communities of faith are urgent in relation to Jews, especially those who live as minorities among Christians. Steps towards assuring non-coercive practices are of highest importance. In dialogue ways should be found for the exchange of concerns, perceptions and safeguards in these matters.

4.4 While Christians agree that there can be no place for coercion of any kind, they do disagree—on the basis of their understandings of the Scriptures—as to what constitutes authentic forms of mission. There is a wide spectrum, from those who see the very presence of the Church in the world as the witness called for, to those who see mission as the explicit and organized proclamation of the gospel to all who have not accepted Jesus as their Savior.

4.5 This spectrum as to mission in general is represented in the different views of what is authentic mission to Jews. Here some of the specifics are as follows: There are Christians who view mission to the Jews as having a very special salvific significance, and those who believe the conversion of the Jews to be the eschatological event that will climax the history of the world. There are those who would place no special emphasis on a mission to the Jews, but would include them in the one mission to all those who have not accepted Christ as their Saviour. There are those who believe that a mission to the Jews is not part of an authentic Christian witness, since the Jewish people finds its fulfillment in faithfulness to God's covenant of old.

25

Christians and Jews Today

In the past, Christians have especially emphasized the differences between their faith and the Jewish faith and have stood aloof from Judaism. Today, the things which Judaism and Christianity have in common are being brought out more and more: Both have grown up out of the soil of the Old Testament-biblical tradition; Jews and Christians believe in the one God; they discover many points of agreement in their worship life, their ethical outlooks, and their view of history.

How did the earlier estrangement and the present discovery of things held in common come about? How should the relationship between Christians and Jews be described today?

Past Estrangement and a New Consciousness

The writings of the New Testament indicate that the first Christian congregations were originally separate communities within Judaism but were eventually no longer tolerated because of their confession of faith in the resurrected Jesus of Nazareth. Then Gentiles began to come into the Christian community through Baptism, without converting to Judaism at the same time. So the Christian community—reluctantly at first—turned to those outside the Jewish people. The result was that Jews and Christians began to see one another as members of two distinct groups rather than as differing voices within Judaism. Even in the New Testament it can be seen how the estrangement of Christians from Jews grew.

215

This development continued in the period which followed. Christianity was elevated to a state religion in the fourth century and gradually became obligatory for all in the Roman Empire. Only the Jews were allowed to continue as a distinct religious community. In this way, however, they fell into the role of the permanent outsiders in Christian lands. People considered them strange and did not understand why they didn't attach themselves to the dominant Christian faith. The result was centuries of persecution.

It was the shock of the Holocaust that brought about a new consciousness. The initiative for a new encounter after 1945 came from both the Christian and the Jewish sides, often from those who had experienced the horrors of the Holocaust themselves or in their own families. Through all of this, Jews and Christians have come to know one another more deeply than at any time since the first century. Out of these encounters grew the firm resolve to organize the relationships between Christians and Jews in such a way that renewed hostility and estrangement could never spring up again.

Is Judaism a World Religion?

Judaism is rightly classified among the world religions. There are Jews in all parts of the world and in most countries on earth. With a total of some 13 million persons, Judaism is numerically the smallest of the great religions. But designating Judaism as a world religion says nothing about its relationship to Christianity. One could get the impression that Judaism is as distant from Christianity as is Hinduism or Buddhism.

For this reason, a smaller group of related religions are often considered together. These are the three "monotheistic world religions," Judaism, Christianity, and Islam. Faith in the one God is their common characteristic. In addition, Jews and Christians have biblical Scriptures in common, and the biblical tradition is also partially accepted in Islam (specifically, the materials about Abraham, Moses, and Jesus). Therefore in our day we often hear the call for a meeting of these religious communities, a trialog. This conversation, however, is still at the earliest stages. Designating Judaism as a world religion clearly does not do justice to the special relationship between Judaism and Christianity.

The Special Relationship between Jews and Christians

Out of the encounters which have taken place since 1945 has emerged the firm resolve that the relationship between Jews and Christians will no more be marked by ignorance and unfamiliarity, but rather by mutual concern and conversation. Jews and Christians belong close together, and in their faith are interrelated. Christians cannot describe their faith without considering its origins in Judaism. It is true that Jews usually say that their faith does not need the link with Christianity; but they also give Christianity a special place because it comes from the same biblical roots. So Jews and Christians find themselves in a dialog concerning their common roots. The close relationship to one another partially explains the bitter estrangement between them, which is reminiscent of a family feud.

The relationship between Christians and Jews can be described by saying they are neighbors. This expresses the fact that ever since Christianity began,

Christians and Jews have existed in spatial and spiritual closeness to one another. However, for long periods of time this was being neighbors at a distance; very often, Christians have not connected the command to love your neighbor with their Jewish neighbors. For this reason, now is the time to recognize one another as neighbors or even as close relatives in faith.

Since they are so closely related, it is appropriate that Jews and Christians care for one another, become acquainted with each other, and meet one another (for example, by reciprocal visits and through studying the Bible together). In such ways the consciousness of belonging together will grow and will express itself in acts of solidarity. Christians and Jews are advised to remain in conversation with one another in a climate of mutual respect, which includes respecting the religious convictions of one another. But it is also essential for genuine meeting that Jews and Christians give to each other an account for the hope that is in them (1 Peter 3:15).

There is no question that the relationship between Christians and Jews which has been described here is only at the beginning of its development. What will come of these efforts, we leave in God's hands. We are already working together so that the differences in belief which exist do not stand in the way of better understanding of one another and of a growing sense of community.

On Regaining the Jewish Roots of Our Tradition

The following excerpts are from "The Significance of Judaism for the Life and Mission of the Church," the Report of the Fourth International Consultation held under the Auspices of the Lutheran World Federation, Department of Studies, in Bossey, Switzerland, August 1982:

- We have learned that the worship, teaching, and preaching of our churches fail in many respects to present an adequate picture of Jews and Judaism. As Christians become more aware of the Jewish roots of their faith, they should make every effort to give expression to this heritage in all fields of the life and work of the church.
- We urge the member churches of the LWF to make a fair and correct presentation of Judaism in all their teaching and preaching. *The Ten Points of Seelisberg* [see pp. 223-224] may serve to alert the churches to areas needing special attention.
- Our liturgies, hymns and prayerbooks make extensive, but selective, use of the Old Testament. We urge that there be an examination of this selection from a theological perspective.
- When we use the Bible we must make sure that old prejudices against the Jews are not repeated. In connection with the public reading of certain passages (e.g. "his blood be on us and on our children"), worship leaders may need to provide appropriate commentary on the original context. Materials written to assist with sermon preparation and private Bible study should also deal sensitively with Jews and the Jewish heritage.
- Unbiased information about the history and persecution of the Jewish people in the post-biblical period, as well as in all subsequent centuries, needs to be included at all levels of the church's educational program. The treatment of Jews and Judaism in all curricular materials needs to be evaluated.
- Teachers of church dogmatics should relate the Christian faith as contained in the ecumenical creeds to its root in

the faith of Israel and to the continuing significance of this common heritage.

- Liturgies can be enriched by a better knowledge of Jewish worship and the festivals known from the Bible and contemporary Judaism.

PART SEVEN

STATEMENTS ON JEWISH-CHRISTIAN RELATIONSHIPS

The Ten Points of Seelisberg

(The following statement, drawn up at a meeting of the International Conference of Christians and Jews in 1947, and addressed to the churches, has become known as *The Ten Points of Seelisberg*.)

1. Remember that One God speaks to us all through the Old and the New Testaments.
2. Remember that Jesus was born of a Jewish mother of the seed of David and the people of Israel, and that His everlasting love and forgiveness embraces His own people and the whole world.
3. Remember that the first disciples, the apostles and the first martyrs were Jews.
4. Remember that the fundamental commandment of Christianity, to love God and one's neighbour, proclaimed already in the Old Testament and confirmed by Jesus, is binding upon both Christians and Jews in all human relationship, without any exception.
5. Avoid distorting or misrepresenting biblical or post-biblical Judaism with the object of extolling Christianity.
6. Avoid using the word *Jews* in the exclusive sense of the enemies of Jesus, and the words *The Enemies of Jesus* to designate the whole Jewish people.
7. Avoid presenting the Passion in such a way as to bring the odium of the killing of Jesus upon all Jews or upon Jews alone. It was only a section of the Jews in Jerusalem who demanded the death of Jesus, and the Christian message has always been that it was the sins of mankind which were exemplified by those Jews and

the sins in which all men share that brought Christ to the Cross.

8. Avoid referring to the scriptural curses, or the cry of a raging mob: *His Blood be Upon Us and Our Children,* without remembering that this cry should not count against the infinitely more weighty words of our Lord: *Father Forgive Them, for They Know not What They Do.*

9. Avoid promoting the superstitious notion that the Jewish people are reprobate, accursed, reserved for a destiny of suffering.

10. Avoid speaking of the Jews as if the first members of the Church had not been Jews.

The American Lutheran Church and the Jewish Community

(A statement of the Seventh General Convention of The American Lutheran Church adopted October 12, 1974, as a statement of comment and counsel addressed to the members of the congregations of The American Lutheran Church to aid them in their decisions and actions.)

Preamble

There are many cogent reasons which urge us to reconsider the relationship of Lutherans, and indeed of all Christians, to Jews. Christians are not as aware as they should be of the common roots and origin of the church and the Jewish tradition of faith and life. Both Judaism and Christianity regard the Hebrew Bible—the Old Testament—as the document which bears witness to the beginning of God's saving work in history. They worship the same God and hold many ethical concerns in common, even though they are divided with respect to faith in Jesus of Nazareth as the Messiah.

Christians must also become aware of that history in which they have deeply alienated the Jews. It is undeniable that Christian people have both initiated and acquiesced in persecution. Whole generations of Christians have looked with contempt upon this people who were condemned to remain wanderers on the earth on the false charge of deicide. Christians ought to acknowledge with repentance and sorrow their part in this tragic history of estrangement. Since anti-Jewish prejudice is still alive in many parts of the world, Christians need to develop a sympathetic understanding of the renewal among Jews of the terror of the Holocaust. It is as if the numbness of the injury has worn off, old wounds have been reopened, and Jews live in dread of another disaster. Christians must join with Jews in the effort to understand the theological and moral significance of what happened in the Holocaust.

We need also to look to the future to see if there are things Christians and Jews can do together in service to the community. Better communication between Christians and Jews can lead to more adequate joint efforts on behalf of a humane society. The new atmosphere in theological research and interfaith encounter which has developed within recent years summons us to undertake serious conversations with Jewish people. Some Christians feel a special concern to explore the contribution which American churches might make in and through contacts with their Jewish neighbors and others to a resolution of the conflict in the Middle East that will be to the benefit of all those living in that region.

The urgency of the foregoing considerations is heightened by the fact that about 50 percent of all Jews live in North America. As Lutherans we ought, therefore, to regard our Jewish neighbors as major partners in the common life.

We urge that Lutherans should understand that their relationship to the Jewish community is one of solidarity, of confrontation, and of respect and cooperation.

I. SOLIDARITY

Our Common Humanity

Lutherans and Jews, indeed all mankind, are united by virtue of their humanity. Lutherans and Jews agree that all people, regardless of race, religion, or nationality are equally God's children, and equally precious in his sight. This conviction is based on a concept of God as Creator of the universe, who continues to care for his creation, whose mercies are over all his creatures.

Our Common Heritage

The existence of Jewish congregations today shows that a religious tradition which traces its ancestry back to the time of Abraham is still living and growing. It is a tradition that gave rise to Christianity; a tradition from which Christianity has borrowed much. But modern Judaism has grown, changed, and developed considerably beyond the Judaism of biblical times, just as the modern church has grown, changed, and developed considerably beyond its New Testament beginnings.

It is unfortunate that so few Christians have studied Judaism as it grew and flowered in the centuries since the New Testament era. The first step for Lutherans, therefore, is to devote themselves to completing this long-neglected homework. It is strongly recommended that Lutherans ask the Jews themselves to teach them about this long and critically important period in Jewish history.

Our Spiritual Solidarity

Our solidarity is based on those ideas and themes held in common, most of which were inherited by Christianity from the Jewish tradition. It is important to note that the ministry of Jesus and the life of the early Christian community were thoroughly rooted in the Judaism of their day. To emphasize the Jewishness of Jesus and his disciples, and to stress all that binds Jews and Christians together in their mutual history, is also to attack one of the sources of anti-Jewish prejudice. We are, after all, brothers one to another. Judaism and Christianity both worship the one God. We both call Abraham father. We both view ourselves as communities covenanted to God. We both feel called to serve in the world as God's witnesses and to be a blessing to mankind.

This emphasis on solidarity is not meant to ignore the many differences that exist between Lutherans and Jews.

Rather it is through an understanding and appreciation of what we have in common that we can best discuss our differences. But for the moment, Lutherans have an obligation to fulfill—namely, to understand adequately and fairly the Jews and Judaism. This is the immediate purpose of Lutheran conversations with Jews.

It is hoped that as Lutherans better understand this similar, yet different religious tradition, the wounds of the past will be healed, and Lutherans and Jews together will be able to face the future receptive to the direction of the Holy Spirit as he seeks to accomplish the will of the One in whom all men live and move and have their being.

II. CONFRONTATION

The History of Separation and Persecution

American Lutherans are the heirs of a long history of prejudicial discrimination against Jews, going back to pre-Christian times. The beginnings of this history of hate are obscure, but gross superstition and the desire for a scapegoat were prominent aspects. The separation between church and synagogue became final by the end of the first century. When Christianity was made the official religion of the Roman empire, a systematic degradation of Jews began in which both church and empire played their parts. Jews were regarded as enemies who were to be eliminated by defamation, extermination, prohibition of their writings, destruction of their synagogues, and exclusion into ghettos and despised occupations. During these 19 centuries, Judaism and Christianity never talked as equals. Disputation and polemics were the media of expression. More recent developments reflect the continuation of patterns of ethnic behavior growing out of this heritage, by which Jews have been excluded by non-Jews, and have, in turn, themselves drawn together in separate communities.

No Christian can exempt himself from involvement in the guilt of Christendom. But Lutherans bear a special responsibility for this tragic history of persecution, because the Nazi movement found a climate of hatred already in existence. The kindness of Scandinavian Lutherans toward Jews cannot alter the ugly facts of forced labor and concentration camps in Hitler's Germany. That the Nazi period fostered a revival of Luther's own medieval hostility toward Jews, as expressed in pugnacious writings, is a special cause of regret. Those who study and admire Luther should acknowledge unequivocally that his anti-Jewish writings are beyond any defense.

In America, Lutherans have been late and lethargic in the struggle for minority rights in the face of inherited patterns of prejudice. We have also been characterized by an inadequate level of ethical sensitivity and action in social and political areas.

Distinctive Ideas, Doctrines, Practices

Customarily, American Lutherans have increased misunderstanding by trying to picture Jews as a "denomination" or "faith-community" like themselves. Actually, Jewishness is both a religious phenomenon and a cultural phenomenon which is exceedingly hard to define. While for most Jews, ancient and modern, it is seen as a matter of physical descent, the aspects of religion and nationhood have at times occupied decisive positions, as is currently true in regard to Zionism. We create misunderstanding when we persist in speaking of "Jewish" creeds and "Jewish" theology, for not all Jews necessarily believe in Judaism, although that religion is their heritage.

Judaism, while it does indeed have teachings, differs markedly from Christian denominations in that its essence is best summed up not in a set of beliefs or creeds, but in a way of life. The distinctive characteristics of the words

"Jew" and "Judaism" should neither be ignored nor should they be revised to fit better with Christian presuppositions. We must rather allow Jewishness to be defined by Jews, and content ourselves with the already tremendous difficulties of trying to keep aware of the complexities of this shifting and not uncontradictory self-understanding.

To the extent that both religious practices and theological reflection manifest themselves among Jews, some basic guidelines can be attempted. There is no reason why Jewish practices and beliefs should be understood or judged differently from those of any minority group. They ought, indeed, to be respected especially by Christians, since they flow from a tradition which served as the "mother" of Christianity. But even where they are in disagreement with the practices and beliefs of Christians, they still deserve the same full protection and support which are given to the religious convictions of any American citizen. While modern interest in ethnicity has furthered the appreciation of diversity of heritages, American Lutherans still need warnings against bigotry and urgings to work toward minority rights.

The unique situation of the sharing of the books of the Hebrew Scriptures by Lutherans and Jews is the source of great problems as well as the potential for significant dialogue. Because Jews are not a "denomination" with a unity shaped by a theological consensus, these Scriptures do not have the same role for them as they do for us. For both Jews and Lutherans the Old Testament has a kind of mediate authority. For Jews this authority is mediated by millennia of tradition and by the individual's choice as to whether or not he will be "religious." For Lutherans as well, the Hebrew Scriptures do not have independent authority. They gain their significance from their role as *Old* Testament and are subordinated to the New Testament Christ, in whom they find a complex fulfillment, involving cancellation as well as acceptance, and reinterpretation as well as reaffirmation. Lutherans must affirm what Jews are free to accept or reject, namely, that it is the same God who reveals himself in both Scriptures. The consequence of this is that Lutherans must view Judaism as a religion with which we in part agree wholeheartedly and yet in part disagree emphatically. Judaism worships the same God as we do (the God of Abraham is our God), yet it disavows the Christ in whom, according to Christian faith, all God's promises have their fulfillment and through whom God has revealed the fullness of his grace.

In view of these divergences, Lutherans and Jews will differ, sometimes drastically, about questions of biblical interpretation, especially in regard to Christian claims about the fulfillment of the Old Testament. Such disagreements should not be the cause of either anger or despair, but rather should be seen as the doorway to a dialogue in which there can occur the discovery of both the real sources of the divergences and their appropriate degree of importance. Out of such learning there can come a mutuality of understanding which can make witness far more meaningful.

III. RESPECT AND COOPERATION

In recognition of the solidarity that unites us and of the tensions and disagreements which have divided us, we affirm the desire of The American Lutheran Church to foster a relationship of respect and cooperation with our Jewish neighbors.

Cooperation in Social Concern

Jews and Lutherans live together in the same society. They have common problems and obligations. The bonds of common citizenship ought to impel Lutherans to take the initiative in promoting friendly relationships and in making common cause with Jews in matters of civic and social concern. It is of special importance that Lutherans demonstrate their commitment to the intrinsic worth of Jewish people by giving them all possible assistance in the struggle against prejudice, discrimination, and persecution. Jews and Lutherans need not share a common creed in order to cooperate to the fullest extent in fostering human rights.

A Mutual Sharing of Faith

Within a context of respect and cooperation, Lutherans should invite Jews to engage in a mutual sharing of convictions. Lutherans who are aware of the Jewish roots of their faith will be moved by both a sense of indebtedness and a desire for deeper understanding to share on the level of religious commitment. Many Lutherans wish to engage in a mutual sharing of convictions, not only for the sake of greater maturity, but also because Christian faith is marked by the impulse to bear witness through word and deed to the grace of God in Jesus Christ.

It is unrealistic to expect that Lutherans will think alike or speak with one voice on the motive and method of bearing witness to their Jewish neighbors. Some Lutherans find in Scripture clear directives to bear missionary witness in which conversion is hoped for. Others hold that when Scripture speaks about the relation between Jews and Christians its central theme is that God's promises to Israel have not been abrogated. The one approach desires to bring Jews into the body of Christ, while the other tends to see the church and the Jewish people as together forming the one people of God, separated from one another for the time being, yet with the promise that they will ultimately become one.

It would be too simple to apply the labels "mission" and "dialogue" to these points of view, although in practice some will want to bear explicit witness through individuals, special societies, or ecclesiastical channels, while others will want to explore the new possibilities of interfaith dialogue. Witness, whether it be called "mission" or "dialogue," includes a desire both to know and to be known more fully. Such witness is intended as a positive, not a negative act. When we speak of a mutual sharing of faith, we are not endorsing a religious syncretism. But we understand that when Lutherans and Jews speak to each other about matters of faith, there will be an exchange which calls for openness, honesty, and mutual respect. One cannot reveal his faith to another without recognizing the real differences that exist and being willing to take the risk of confronting these differences.

We wish to stress the importance of interfaith dialogue as a rich opportunity for growth in mutual understanding and for a new grasp of our common potentiality for service to humanity. We commend to The American Lutheran Church the LCUSA [Lutheran Council in the U.S.A.] document, "Some Observations and Guidelines for Conversations between Lutherans and Jews," as a helpful means toward realizing the goals of interfaith dialogue. It should be understood that the LCUSA document limits itself to the aims and methods of dialogue and does not attempt to cover the entire field of Lutheran-Jewish relationships. Consequently, its comment that "neither polemics nor conversions are the aim of such conversations" does not rule out mission.

The State of Israel

The LCUSA "Guidelines" wisely suggest that "the State of Israel" be one of the topics for Jewish-Lutheran conversations. The tragic encounter of two peoples in the Middle East places a heavy responsibility upon Lutherans to be concerned about the legitimacy of the Jewish state, the rights of the Palestinians, and the problems of all refugees.

The history and circumstances of the Israeli-Arab conflict are very complicated. It is understandable that Lutherans should be deeply divided in their evaluation of the situation in the Middle East. In Jewish opinion, Israel is more than another nation. It is a symbol of resurrection following upon the near extinction of the Jewish people within living memory. There are also some Lutherans who find a religious significance in the State of Israel, seeing in recent events a fulfillment of biblical promises. Other Lutherans espouse not a "theology of the land," but a "theology of the poor," with special reference to the plight of the Palestinian refugees. Still other Lutherans endorse what might be called a "theology of human survival," believing that the validity of the State of Israel rests on juridical and moral grounds.

It seems clear that there is no consensus among Lutherans with respect to the relation between the "chosen people" and the territory comprising the present State of Israel. But there should be a consensus with respect to our obligation to appreciate, in a spirit of repentance for past misdeeds and silences, the factors which gave birth to the State of Israel and to give prayerful attention to the circumstances that bear on the search for Jewish and Arab security and dignity in the Middle East.

Ecumenical Considerations on Jewish-Christian Dialogue

(Received and commended to the churches for study and action by the Executive Committee of the World Council of Churches, Geneva, July 1982.)

Preface

1.1   One of the functions of dialogue is to allow participants to describe and witness to their faith in their own terms. This is of primary importance since self-serving descriptions of other peoples' faith are one of the roots of prejudice, stereotyping, and condescension. Listening carefully to the neighbours' self-understanding enables Christians better to obey the commandment not to bear false witness against their neighbours, whether those neighbours be of long-established religious, cultural or ideological traditions or members of new religious groups. It should be recognized by partners in dialogue that any religion or ideology claiming universality, apart from having an understanding of itself, will also have its own interpretations of other religions and ideologies as part of its own self-understanding. Dialogue gives an opportunity for a mutual questioning of the understanding partners have about themselves and others. It is out of a reciprocal willingness to listen and learn that significant dialogue grows. (WCC Guidelines on Dialogue, III.4)

1.2   In giving such guidelines applicable to all dialogues, the World Council of Churches speaks primarily to its member churches as it defines the need for and gifts to be received by dialogue. People of other faiths may choose to define their understanding of dialogue, and their expectations as to how dialogue with Christians may affect their own traditions and attitudes and may lead to a better understanding of Christianity. Fruitful "mutual questioning of the understanding partners have about themselves and others" requires the spirit of dialogue. But the WCC Guidelines do not predict what partners in dialogue may come to learn about themselves, their history, and their problems. Rather they speak within the churches about faith, attitudes, actions, and problems of Christians.

1.3   In all dialogues distinct asymmetry between any two communities of faith becomes an important fact. Already terms like faith, theology, religion, Scripture, people, etc. are not innocent or neutral. Partners in dialogue may rightly question the very language in which each thinks about religious matters.

1.4   In the case of Jewish-Christian dialogue a specific historical and theological asymmetry is obvious. While an understanding of Judaism in New Testament times becomes an integral and indispensable part of any Christian theology, for Jews, a "theological" understanding of Christianity is of a less than essential or integral significance. Yet, neither community of faith has developed without awareness of the other.

1.5   The relations between Jews and Christians have unique characteristics because of the ways in which Christianity historically emerged out of Judaism. Christian understandings of that process constitute a necessary part of the dialogue and give urgency to the enterprise. As Christianity came to define its own identity over against Judaism, the Church developed its own understandings, definitions and terms for what it had inherited from Jewish traditions, and for what it read in the Scriptures common to Jews and Christians. In the process of defining its own identity the Church defined Judaism, and assigned to the Jews definite

236

roles in its understanding of God's acts of salvation. It should not be surprising that Jews resent those Christian theologies in which they as a people are assigned to play a negative role. Tragically, such patterns of thought in Christianity have often led to overt acts of condescension, persecutions, and worse.

1.6   Bible-reading and worshipping Christians often believe that they "know Judaism" since they have the Old Testament, the records of Jesus' debates with Jewish teachers and the early Christian reflections on the Judaism of their times. Furthermore, no other religious tradition has been so thoroughly "defined" by preachers and teachers in the Church as has Judaism. This attitude is often enforced by lack of knowledge about the history of Jewish life and thought through the 1,900 years since the parting of the ways of Judaism and Christianity.

1.7   For these reasons there is special urgency for Christians to listen, through study and dialogue, to ways in which Jews understand their history and their traditions, their faith and their obedience "in their own terms". Furthermore, a mutual listening to how each is perceived by the other may be a step towards understanding the hurts, overcoming the fears, and correcting the misunderstandings that have thrived on isolation.

1.8   Both Judaism and Christianity comprise a wide spectrum of opinions, options, theologies, and styles of life and service. Since generalizations often produce stereotyping, Jewish-Christian dialogue becomes the more significant by aiming at as full as possible a representation of views within the two communities of faith.

2. Towards a Christian Understanding of Jews and Judaism

2.1   Through dialogue with Jews many Christians have come to appreciate the richness and vitality of Jewish faith and life in the covenant and have been enriched in their own understandings of God and the divine will for all creatures.

2.2   In dialogue with Jews, Christians have learned that the actual history of Jewish faith and experiences does not match the images of Judaism that have dominated a long history of Christian teaching and writing, images that have been spread by Western culture and literature into other parts of the world.

2.3   A classical Christian tradition sees the Church replacing Israel as God's people, and the destruction of the second temple of Jerusalem as a warrant for this claim. The covenant of God with the people of Israel was only a preparation for the coming of Christ, after which it was abrogated.

2.4   Such a theological perspective has had fateful consequences. As the Church replaced the Jews as God's people, the Judaism that survived was seen as a fossilized religion of legalism—a view now perpetuated by scholarship which claims no theological interests. Judaism of the first centuries before and after the birth of Jesus was therefore called "Late Judaism". The Pharisees were considered to represent the acme of legalism, Jews and Jewish groups were portrayed as negative models, and the truth and beauty of Christianity were thought to be enhanced by setting up Judaism as false and ugly.

2.5   Through a renewed study of Judaism and in dialogue with Jews, Christians have become aware that Judaism in the time of Christ was in an early stage of its long life. Under the leadership of the Pharisees the Jewish people began a spiritual revival of remarkable power, which gave them the vitality capable of surviving the catastrophe of the loss of the temple. It gave birth to Rabbinic Judaism which produced the Mishnah and Talmud and built the structures for a strong and creative life through the centuries.

2.6   As a Jew, Jesus was born into this tradition. In that setting he was nurtured by the Hebrew Scriptures, which he accepted as authoritative and to which he gave a new interpretation in his life and teaching. In this context Jesus announced that the Kingdom of God was at hand, and in his resurrection his followers found the confirmation of his being both Lord and Messiah.

2.7   Christians should remember that some of the controversies reported in the New Testament between Jesus and the "scribes and Pharisees" find parallels within Pharisaism itself and its heir, Rabbinic Judaism. These controversies took place in a Jewish context, but when the words of Jesus came to be used by Christians who did not identify with the Jewish people as Jesus did, such sayings often became weapons in anti-Jewish polemics and thereby their original intention was tragically distorted. An internal Christian debate is now taking place on the question of how to understand passages in the New Testament that seem to contain anti-Jewish references.

2.8   Judaism, with its rich history of spiritual life, produced the Talmud as the normative guide for Jewish life in thankful response to the grace of God's covenant with the people of Israel. Over the centuries important commentaries, profound philosophical works and poetry of spiritual depth have been added. For Judaism the Talmud is central and authoritative. Judaism is more than the religion of the Scriptures of Israel. What Christians call the Old Testament has received in the Talmud and later writings interpretations that for Jewish tradition share in the authority of Moses.

2.9   For Christians the Bible with the two Testaments is also followed by traditions of interpretation, from the Church Fathers to the present time. Both Jews and Christians live in the continuity of their Scripture and Tradition.

2.10   Christians as well as Jews look to the Hebrew Bible as the story recording Israel's sacred memory of God's election and covenant with this people. For Jews, it is their own story in historical continuity with the present. Christians, mostly of gentile background since early in the life of the Church, believe themselves to be heirs to this same story by grace in Jesus Christ. The relationship between the two communities, both worshipping the God of Abraham, Isaac and Jacob, is a given historical fact, but how it is to be understood theologically is a matter of internal discussion among Christians, a discussion that can be enriched by dialogue with Jews.

2.11   Both commonalities and differences between the two faiths need to be examined carefully. Finding in the Scriptures of the Old and New Testaments the authority sufficient for salvation, the Christian Church shares Israel's faith in the One God, whom it knows in the Spirit as the God and Father of the Lord Jesus Christ. For Christians, Jesus Christ is the only begotten Son of the Father, through whom millions have come to share in the love of, and to adore, the God who first made covenant with the people of Israel. Knowing the One God in Jesus Christ through the Spirit, therefore, Christians worship that God with a Trinitarian confession to the One God, the God of Creation, Incarnation and Pentecost. In so doing, the Church worships in a language foreign to Jewish worship and sensitivities, yet full of meaning to Christians.

2.12   Christians and Jews both believe that God has created men and women as the crown of creation and has called them to be holy and to exercise stewardship over the creation in accountability to God. Jews and Christians are taught by their Scriptures and Traditions to know themselves responsible to their neighbours especially to those who are weak, poor and oppressed. In various and distinct ways they look for the day in which God will redeem the creation. In dialogue with Jews many Christians come to a more profound appreciation of the Exodus hope of liberation, and pray and work for the coming of righteousness and peace on earth.

2.13   Christians learn through dialogue with Jews that for Judaism the survival of the Jewish people is inseparable from its obedience to God and God's covenant.

2.14   During long periods, both before and after the emergence of Christianity, Jews found ways of living in obedience to Torah, maintaining and deepening their calling as a peculiar people in the midst of the nations. Through history there are times and places in which Jews were allowed to live, respected and accepted by the cultures in which they resided, and where their own culture thrived and made a distinct and sought after contribution to their Christian and Muslim neighbours. Often lands not dominated by Christians proved most favorable for Jewish diaspora living. There were even times when Jewish thinkers came to "make a virtue out of necessity" and considered diaspora living to be the distinct genius of Jewish existence.

2.15   Yet, there was no time in which the memory of the Land of Israel and of Zion, the city of Jerusalem, was not central in the worship and hope of the Jewish people. "Next year in Jerusalem" was always part of Jewish worship in the diaspora. And the continued presence of Jews in the Land and in Jerusalem was always more than just one place of residence among all the others.

2.16   Jews differ in their interpretations of the State of Israel, as to its religious and secular meaning. It constitutes for them part of the long search for that survival which has always been central to Judaism through the ages. Now the quest for statehood by Palestinians—Christian and Muslim—as part of their search for survival as a people in the Land—also calls for full attention.

2.17   Jews, Christians and Muslims have all maintained a presence in the Land from their beginnings. While "the Holy Land" is primarily a Christian designation, the Land is holy to all three. Although they may understand its holiness in different ways, it cannot be said to be "more holy" to one than to another.

2.18   The need for dialogue is the more urgent when under strain the dialogue is tested. Is it mere debate and negotiation or is it grounded in faith that God's will for the world is secure peace with justice and compassion?

3. Hatred and Persecution of Jews—A Continuing Concern

3.1   Christians cannot enter into dialogue with Jews without the awareness that hatred and persecution of Jews have a long persistent history, especially in countries where Jews constitute a minority among Christians. The tragic history of the persecution of Jews includes massacres in Europe and the Middle East by the Crusaders, the Inquisition, pogroms, and the Holocaust. The World Council of Churches Assembly at its first meeting in Amsterdam, 1948, declared: "We call upon the churches we represent to denounce antisemitism, no matter what its origin, as absolutely irreconcilable with the profession and practice of the Christian faith. Antisemitism is sin against God and man". This appeal has been reiterated many times. Those who live where there is a record of acts of hatred against Jews can serve the whole Church by unmasking the ever-present danger they have come to recognize.

3.2   Teachings of contempt for Jews and Judaism in certain Christian traditions proved a spawning ground for the evil of the Nazi Holocaust. The Church must learn so to preach and teach the Gospel as to make sure that it cannot be used towards contempt for Judaism and against the Jewish people. A further response to the Holocaust by Christians, and one which is shared by their Jewish partners, is a resolve that it will never happen again to the Jews or to any other people.

3.3   Discrimination against and persecution of Jews have deep-rooted socio-economic and political aspects. Religious differences are magnified to justify ethnic hatred in support of vested interests. Similar phenomena are also evident in many interracial conflicts. Christians should oppose all such religious prejudices, whereby people are made scapegoats for the failures and problems of societies and political regimes.

3.4 Christians in parts of the world with a history of little or no persecution of Jews do not wish to be conditioned by the specific experiences of justified guilt among other Christians. Rather, they explore in their own ways the significance of Jewish-Christian relations, from the earliest times to the present, for their life and witness.

4. *Authentic Christian Witness*

4.1 Christians are called to witness to their faith in word and deed. The Church has a mission and it cannot be otherwise. This mission is not one of choice.

4.2 Christians have often distorted their witness by coercive proselytism—conscious and unconscious, overt and subtle. Referring to proselytism between Christian churches, the Joint Working Group of the Roman Catholic Church and the World Council of Churches stated: "Proselytism embraces whatever violates the right of the human person, Christian or non-Christians, to be free from external coercion in religious matters". (*Ecumenical Review,* 1/1971, p. 11)

4.3 Such rejection of proselytism, and such advocacy of respect for the integrity and the identity of all persons and all communities of faith are urgent in relation to Jews, especially those who live as minorities among Christians. Steps towards assuring non-coercive practices are of highest importance. In dialogue ways should be found for the exchange of concerns, perceptions, and safeguards in these matters.

4.4   While Christians agree that there can be no place for coercion of any kind, they do disagree—on the basis of their understandings of the Scriptures—as to what constitutes authentic forms of mission. There is a wide spectrum, from those who see the very presence of the Church in the world as the witness called for, to those who see mission as the explicit and organized proclamation of the gospel to all who have not accepted Jesus as their Saviour.

4.5   This spectrum as to mission in general is represented in the different views of what is authentic mission to Jews. Here some of the specifics are as follows: There are Christians who view a mission to the Jews as having a very special salvific significance, and those who believe the conversion of the Jews to be the eschatological event that will climax the history of the world. There are those who would place no special emphasis on a mission to the Jews, but would include them in the one mission to all those who have not accepted Christ as their Saviour. There are those who believe that a mission to the Jews is not part of an authentic Christian witness, since the Jewish people finds its fulfillment in faithfulness to God's covenant of old.

4.6   Dialogue can rightly be described as a mutual witness, but only when the intention is to hear the others in order better to understand their faith, hopes, insights, and concerns, and to give, to the best of one's ability one's own understanding of one's own faith. The spirit of dialogue is to be fully present to one another in full openness and human vulnerability.

4.7   According to rabbinic law, Jews who confess Jesus as the Messiah are considered apostate Jews. But for many Christians of Jewish origin, their identification with the Jewish people is a deep spiritual reality to which they seek to give expression in various ways, some by observing parts of Jewish tradition in worship and life-style, many by a special commitment to the well-being of the Jewish people and to a peaceful and secure future for the State of Israel. Among Christians of Jewish origin there is the same wide spectrum of attitudes towards mission as among other Christians, and the same criteria for dialogue and against coercion apply.

4.8   As Christians of different traditions enter into dialogue with Jews in local, national, and international situations, they will come to express their understanding of Judaism in other language, style, and ways than has been done in these Ecumenical Considerations. Such understandings are to be shared among the churches for enrichment of all.

Nostra Aetate

(This declaration by the Second Vatican Council in October 1965 is part of the "Declaration on the Relationship of the Church to Non-Christian Religions.")

As this Sacred Synod searches into the mystery of the Church, it remembers the bond that spiritually ties the people of the New Covenant to Abraham's stock.

Thus the Church of Christ acknowledges that, according to God's saving design, the beginnings of her faith and her election are found already among the Patriachs, Moses and the prophets. She professes that all who believe in Christ—Abraham's sons according to faith—are included in the same Patriarch's call, and likewise that the salvation of the Church is mysteriously foreshadowed by the chosen people's exodus from the land of bondage. The Church, therefore, cannot forget that she received the revelation of the Old Testament through the people with whom God in His inexpressible mercy concluded the Ancient Covenant. Nor can she forget that she draws sustenance from the root of that well-cultivated olive tree onto which has been grafted the wild shoot, the Gentiles. Indeed, the Church believes that by His cross Christ Our Peace reconciled Jews and Gentiles, making both one in Himself.

The Church keeps ever in mind the words of the Apostle about his kinsmen: "Theirs is the sonship and the glory and the covenants and the law and the worship and the promises; theirs are the fathers and from them is the Christ according to the flesh" (Rom. 9:4-5), the Son of the Virgin Mary. She also recalls that the Apostles, the Church's mainstay and pillars, as well as most of the early disciples who proclaimed Christ's Gospel to the world, sprang from the Jewish people.

As Holy Scripture testifies, Jerusalem did not recognize the time of her visitation, nor did the Jews, in large number, accept the Gospel; indeed not a few opposed its spreading. Nevertheless God holds the Jews most dear for the sake of their Fathers; He does not repent of the gifts He makes or of the calls He issues—such is the witness of the Apostle. In company with the Prophets and the same Apostle, the Church awaits that day, known to God alone, on which all peoples will address the Lord in a single voice and "serve him shoulder to shoulder" (Soph. 3:9).

Since the spiritual patrimony common to Christians and Jews is thus so great, this Sacred Synod wants to foster and recommend that mutual understanding and respect which is the fruit, above all, of biblical and theological studies as well as of fraternal dialogues.

True, the Jewish authorities and those who followed their lead pressed for the death of Christ; still, what happened in His passion cannot be charged against all the Jews, without distinction, then alive, nor against the Jews of today. Although the Church is the new people of God, the Jews should not be presented as rejected or accursed by God, as if this followed from the Holy Scriptures. All should see to it, then, that in catechetical work or in the preaching of the word of God they do not teach anything that does not conform to the truth of the Gospel and the spirit of Christ.

Furthermore, in her rejection of every persecution against any man, the Church, mindful of the patrimony she shares with the Jews and moved not by political reasons but by the Gospel's spiritual love, decries hatred, persecutions, displays of anti-Semitism, directed against Jews at any time and by anyone.

Besides, as the Church has always held and holds now, Christ underwent His passion and death freely, because of the sins of men and out of infinite love, in order that all may reach salvation. It is, therefore, the burden of the Church's preaching to proclaim the cross of Christ as the sign of God's all-embracing love and as the fountain from which every grace flows.

Guidelines and Suggestions for Implementing the Conciliar Declaration Nostra Aetate

(These guidelines and suggestions were issued by the Vatican Commission for Religious Relations with the Jews in January 1975.)

The Declaration Nostra Aetate, issued by the Second Vatican Council on October 28, 1965, "On the Relationship of the Church to Non-Christian Religions" (n. 4), marks an important milestone in the history of Jewish-Christians relations.

Moreover, the step taken by the Council finds its historical setting in circumstances deeply affected by the memory of the persecution and massacre of Jews which took place in Europe just before and during the Second World War.

Although Christianity sprang from Judaism, taking from it certain essential elements of its faith and divine cult, the gap dividing them was deepened more and more, to such an extent that Christian and Jew hardly knew each other.

After two thousand years, too often marked by mutual ignorance and frequent confrontation, the Declaration *Nostra Aetate* provides an opportunity to open or to continue a dialogue with a view to better mutual understanding. Over the past nine years, many steps in this direction have been taken in various countries. As a result, it is easier to distinguish the conditions under which a new relationship between Jews and Christians may be worked out and developed. This seems the right moment to propose, following the guidelines of the Council, some concrete suggestions born of experience, hoping that they will help to bring into actual existence in the life of the Church the intentions expressed in the conciliar document.

While referring the reader back to this document, we may simply restate here that the spiritual bonds and historical links binding the Church to Judaism condemn (as opposed to the very spirit of Christianity) all forms of anti-Semitism and discrimination, which in any case the dignity of the human person alone would suffice to condemn. Further still, these links and relationships render obligatory a better mutual understanding and renewed mutual esteem. On the practical level in particular, Christians must therefore strive to acquire a better knowledge of the basic components of the religious tradition of Judaism: they must strive to learn by what essential traits the Jews define themselves in the light of their own religious experience.

With due respect for such matters of principle, we simply propose some first practical applications in different essential areas of the Church's life, with a view to launching or developing sound relations between Catholics and their Jewish brothers.

Dialogue

To tell the truth, such relations as there have been between Jew and Christian have scarcely ever risen above the level of monologue. From now on, real dialogue must be established.

Dialogue presupposes that each side wishes to know the other, and wishes to increase and deepen its knowledge of the other. It constitutes a particularly suitable means of favoring a better mutual knowledge and, especially in the case of dialogue between Jews and Christians, of probing the riches of one's own tradition. Dialogue demands respect for the other as he is; above all, respect for his faith and his religious convictions.

In virtue of her divine mission, and her very nature, the Church must preach Jesus Christ to the world (*Ad Gentes*, 2). Lest the witness of Catholics to Jesus Christ should give offense to Jews, they must take care to live and spread their Christian faith while maintaining the strictest respect for religious liberty, in line with the teaching of the Second Vatican Council (Declaration *Dignitatis Humanae*). They will likewise strive to understand the difficulties which arise for the Jewish soul—rightly imbued with an extremely high, pure notion of the divine transcendence—when faced with the mystery of the incarnate Word.

While it is true that a widespread air of suspicion, inspired by an unfortunate past, is still dominant in this particular area, Christians for their part, will be able to see to what extent the responsibility is theirs and deduce practical conclusions for the future.

In addition to friendly talks, competent people will be encouraged to meet and to study together the many problems deriving from the fundamental convictions of Judaism and of Christianity. In order not to hurt (even involuntarily) those taking part, it will be vital to guarantee, not only tact, but a great openness of spirit and diffidence with respect to one's own prejudices.

In whatever circumstances as shall prove possible and mutually acceptable, one might encourage a common meeting in the presence of God, in prayer and silent meditation, a highly efficacious way of finding that humility, that openness of heart and mind, necessary prerequisites for a deep knowledge of oneself and of others. In particular, that will be done in connection with great causes, such as the struggle for peace and justice.

Liturgy

The existing links between the Christian liturgy and the Jewish liturgy will be borne in mind. The idea of a living community in the service of God, and in the service of men for the love of God, such as it is realized in the liturgy, is just as characteristic of the Jewish liturgy as it is of the Christian one. To improve Jewish-Christian relations, it is important to take cognizance of those common elements of the liturgical life (formulas, feasts, rites, etc.) in which the Bible holds an essential place.

An effort will be made to acquire a better understanding of whatever in the Old Testament retains its own perpetual value (cf. *Dei Verbum,* 14-15), since that has not been cancelled by the later interpretation of the New Testament. Rather, the New Testament brings out the full meaning of the Old, while both Old and New illumine and explain each other (cf. *ibid.,* 16). This is all the more important since liturgical reform is now bringing the text of the Old Testament ever more frequently to the attention of Christians.

When commenting on biblical texts, emphasis will be laid on the continuity of our faith with that of the earlier Covenant, in the perspective of the promises, without minimizing those elements of Christianity which are original. We believe that those promises were fulfilled with the first coming of Christ. But it is nonetheless true that we still await their perfect fulfillment in His glorious return at the end of time.

With respect to liturgical readings, care will be taken to see that homilies based on them will not distort their meaning, especially when it is a question of passages which seem to show the Jewish people as such in an unfavorable light. Efforts will be made so to instruct the Christian people that they will understand the true interpretation of all the texts and their meaning for the contemporary believer.

Commissions entrusted with the task of liturgical translation will pay particular attention to the way in which they express those phrases and passages which Christians, if not well informed, might misunderstand because of prejudice. Obviously, one cannot alter the text of the Bible. The point is that, with a version destined for liturgical use, there should be an overriding preoccupation to bring out explicitly the meaning of a text, while taking scriptural studies into account. (Thus the formula "the Jews," in St. John, sometimes according to the context means "the leaders of the Jews," or "the adversaries of Jesus," terms which express better the thought of the Evangelist and avoid appearing to arraign the Jewish people as such. Another example is the use of the words "Pharisee" and "Pharisaism", which have taken on a largely pejorative meaning.)

The preceding remarks also apply to the introductions to biblical readings, to the Prayer of the Faithful, and to commentaries printed in missals used by the laity.

Teaching and Education

Although there is still a great deal of work to be done, a better understanding of Judaism itself and its relationship to Christianity has been achieved in recent years thanks to the teaching of the Church, the study and research of scholars, as also to the beginning of dialogue. In this respect, the following facts deserve to be recalled:

It is the same God, "inspirer and author of the books of both Testaments" (*Dei Verbum,* 16), Who speaks both in the old and new Covenants.

Judaism in the time of Christ and the Apostles was a complex reality, embracing many different trends, many spiritual, religious, social, and cultural values.

The Old Testament and the Jewish tradition founded upon it must not be set against the New Testament in such a way that the former seems to constitute a religion of only justice, fear, and legalism, with no appeal to the love of God and neighbor (cf. Dt 6:5; Lv 19:18; Mt 22:34-40).

Jesus was born of the Jewish people, as were His apostles and a large number of His first disciples. When He revealed Himself as the Messiah and Son (cf. Mt 16:16), the bearer of the new Gospel message, He did so as the fulfillment and perfection of the earlier Revelation. And although His teaching had a profoundly new character, Christ, nevertheless, in many instances, took His stand on the teaching of the Old Testament. The New Testament is profoundly marked by its relation to the Old. As the Second Vatican Council declared: "God, the inspirer and author of the books of both Testaments, wisely arranged that the New Testament be hidden in the Old and the Old be made manifest in the New" (*Dei Verbum,* 16). Jesus also used teaching methods similar to those employed by the rabbis of His time.

With regard to the trial and death of Jesus, the Council recalled that "what happened in His passion cannot be blamed upon all the Jews then living, without distinction, nor upon the Jews of today" (*Nostra Aetate*).

The history of Judaism did not end with the destruction of Jerusalem, but rather went on to develop a religious tradition. And, although we believe that the importance and meaning of that tradition were deeply affected by the coming of Christ, it is nonetheless rich in religious values.

With the prophets and the apostle Paul, "the Church awaits the day, known to God alone, on which all peoples will address the Lord in a single voice and serve Him with one accord (Soph 3:9)" (*Nostra Aetate*).

Information concerning these questions is important at all levels of Christian instruction and education. Among sources of information, special attention should be paid to the following: catechisms and religious textbooks, history books, the mass media (press, radio, movies, television).

The effective use of these means presupposes the thorough formation of instructors and educators in training schools, seminaries, and universities.

Research into the problems bearing on Judaism and Jewish-Christian relations will be encouraged among specialists, particularly in the fields of exegesis, theology, history, and sociology. Higher institutions of Catholic research, in association if possible with other similar Christian institutions and experts, are invited to contribute to the solution of such problems. Wherever possible, chairs of Jewish studies will be created, and collaboration with Jewish scholars encouraged.

Joint Social Action

Jewish and Christian tradition, founded on the word of God, is aware of the value of the human person, the image of God. Love of the same God must show itself in effective action for the good of mankind. In the spirit of the prophets, Jews and Christians will work willingly together, seeking social justice and peace at every level—local, national, and international.

At the same time, such collaboration can do much to foster mutual understanding and esteem.

Conclusion

The Second Vatican Council has pointed out the path to follow in promoting deep fellowship between Jews and Christians. But there is still a long road ahead.

The problem of Jewish-Christian relations concerns the Church as such, since it is when "pondering her own mystery" that she encounters the mystery of Israel. Therefore, even in areas where no Jewish communities exist, this remains an important problem. There is also an ecumenical aspect to the question: the very return of Christians to the sources and origins of their faith, grafted onto the earlier Covenant, helps the search for unity in Christ, the cornerstone.

In this field, the bishops will know what best to do on the pastoral level, within the general disciplinary framework of the Church and in line with the common teaching of her magisterium. For example, they will create some suitable commissions or secretariats on a national or regional level, or appoint some competent person to promote the implementation of the conciliar directives and the suggestions made above.

On October 22, 1974, the Holy Father instituted for the universal Church this Commission for Religious Relations with the Jews, joined to the Secretariat for promoting Christian Unity. This special Commission, created to encourage and foster religious relations between Jews and Catholics—and to do so eventually in collaboration with other Christians—will be, within the limits of its competence, at the service of all interested organizations, providing information for them, and helping them to pursue their task in conformity with the instructions of the Holy See.

Suggestions for Group Study

Chapter 1: The Jews in North America

1. What do you think accounts for the fact that the influence of Jews in the United States and Canada far surpasses their numbers? (Only 2.5% of the U.S. population is Jewish, yet numerous Jewish persons are prominent in politics, science, and the arts.)

2. How would you describe the different approaches of Reform and Conservative Judaism? What might be some reasons why Conservative Judaism has become more dominant in North America than Reform Judaism?

3. Did the percentages of Jews in the United States who are nonaffiliated, Orthodox, Reform, and Conservative surprise you? Why do you suppose so many have no relationship to a synagogue?

Chapter 2: An Outline of Jewish History

1. Three parties or groups were in existence in Judaism at the time of Jesus: the Pharisees, the Essenes, and the Sadducees. Had you heard of all three before? What do you know about them?

2. The history of the Jews from the fourth century onward has been characterized by varying degrees of persecution. Why do you think that the Crusades during the Middle Ages led to increased persecution?

3. What do you think has made it possible for the Jewish people to maintain their identity and tradition in spite of all the hatred and persecution that has been directed against them down through history?

Chapter 3: Israel: Not Just a Country

1. Why is it a mistake to equate the State of Israel with the Jewish people? What role does the State of Israel have in modern Judaism?

2. Christians have sometimes used the name *Israel* to mean the community of those who have faith in Jesus Christ—a new people of God made up of both Jews and Gentiles. Do you think this is an appropriate use of the term *Israel*? Why or why not?

3. How would you compare or contrast *The Israel Declaration of Independence* with the U.S. *Declaration of Independence?* How would you describe the goals and ideals expressed in the two documents?

Chapter 4: The Land of Israel

1. The Jewish people have always had strong feelings about the land of Israel. Have you or people you have known felt a strong link to a certain place? How do you think such ties to particular places develop? How did they develop for the Jews?

2. What do you think of the statement that "The land was God's gift to God's people, but it was never Israel's irrevocable possession to be used however they wished" (p. 52). What can happen when any of us misuses God's gifts?

3. The book says that "the New Testament's restraint in speaking of the land's significance for the faith should be observed" (pp. 55-56). Discuss why Jews and Christians place somewhat different emphases on the importance of the Holy Land.

Chapter 5: Zionism

1. What are some of the historical reasons why Zionism has become a powerful force among Jews today? Do you think the policies of the State of Israel today have remained

consistent with the principles of Zionism and with the *Israel Declaration of Independence* (see pp. 48-50)?

2. What do you think about the 1975 declaration by the United Nations General Assembly that Zionism is "a form of racism"? Do you agree with the statement that "it is all too easy for the old, anti-Semitic ideology to lurk behind" the banner of anti-Zionism?

3. The conflicting claims over the land and over equal rights for all citizens of the State of Israel cause concern for Christians. What are some steps Christians can take that might be helpful?

Chapter 6: Jerusalem

1. How much attachment should Christians feel toward Jerusalem as a physical location? To what degree does one's religious attachment to a place (such as Golgotha, the Dome of the Rock, or the "Wailing Wall") give one the right to help determine how that place is governed or cared for?

2. Does it surprise you that Judaism continued to be an important world religion after the destruction of the temple in A.D. 70 and the end of the sacrificial system? What do you think enabled Judaism to thrive in spite of this catastrophe?

3. Christians often think of Jerusalem as a heavenly entity instead of as an earthly reality. What does the word *Jerusalem* mean to you?

Chapter 7: Religious Movements

1. What are some of the differences between Sephardic and Ashkenazic Judaism (origins, language, and so forth)?

2. Which of the three principal Jewish movements (Orthodox, Reform, and Conservative) is the most willing to adapt Jewish tradition to changing circumstances? What are some benefits and dangers in adapting a religious tradition to fit modern situations?

3. Orthodox Judaism holds firmly to tradition in spite of changes in society. Do you think this will prove to be a strength or a weakness over a long period of time?

Chapter 8: Jewish Prayer

1. The text states that for the devout Jew, the whole of life is worship. Do you think this consists of many prayers throughout the day, or an attitude of trusting oneself to God, or both?

2. What are some of the similarities between Jewish and Christian prayer? What are some of the differences?

3. Scan the *Amidah* (pp. 86-89). Which words or phrases remind you of the Lord's Prayer?

Chapter 9: The Jewish Festival Year

1. Has anyone in the group been a guest in a Jewish synagogue or home for a Jewish festival celebration? If so, have that person share his or her impressions of the experience.

2. What connections do you see between the Passover meal and the Lord's Supper? (Note that these will be discussed in more detail in Chapter 19.)

3. The festival of Yom Kippur includes the private making of amends and requests for forgiveness as well as the congregational confession of sins. Does your congregation encourage some form of private confession? Do you think private confession would be helpful as a regular part of Christian life?

Chapter 10: Celebrations in the Home

1. The book states that "a Jewish family can practice a fully authentic worship life in home celebrations, even if it is not possible for them to worship in a synagogue." Would this be possible for a Christian family?

2. What did you find most striking about the various steps in the observance of the Sabbath in the home by devout Jews?

3. What are some of the benefits and advantages of home worship? How could some of these strengths be built into observances of Christian festivals?

Chapter 11: *Rites of Passage*

1. What is the purpose of the Bar Mitzvah (Bat Mitzvah for girls)? How is it similar to and different from the Christian practice of confirmation?

2. What are your impressions of the various parts of the Jewish wedding service? What are some similarities and differences between that service and a Christian wedding ceremony?

3. Jewish mourning customs include the use of a plain, white garment for burial, a simple coffin, and no flowers— since in death all are equal. Do you see any advantages in this custom? Would you approve of such a simple funeral for yourself or your family members? Why or why not?

Chapter 12: *Worship in the Synagogue*

1. The Torah scrolls are always kept in the front of the worship area in a synagogue. What do you think is the reason for this? What objects do Christian churches usually have in the front of a church? Are they placed there for similar reasons?

2. What aspects of Jewish worship would be unfamiliar to most Christians? What aspects seem unusual to you?

3. What are some similarities between Jewish and Christian worship? What aspects of Jewish worship would seem familiar to you?

Chapter 13: The Content of Jewish Faith

1. Do you agree with the statement that Christians are mainly concerned about doctrinal uniformity? Why or why not?

2. Since the *Shema* is the most fundamental confession of Jewish faith, why might many Jews find the Christian doctrine of the Trinity blasphemous? How do Christians explain the fact that they worship "three persons in one God"?

3. The book states that "In working out Christian conduct, with the Ten Commandments as the basis, Christians are given a great deal of freedom for individual decision and responsibility before God." How much specific direction do you seek out from the Bible when making decisions?

Chapter 14: The Pharisees

1. The apostle Paul was a Pharisee taught by Gamaliel, who was of the school of Hillel. Read Acts 5:34-39, especially vv. 38-39, to see what Gamaliel said about Christianity. What do you think of his advice? Does it fit the stereotype of what the Pharisees were like?

2. Many times the New Testament (especially the gospel of John) refers to the enemies of Jesus by using the phrase, "the Jews." Why is it so dangerous for Christians to apply such New Testament passages to all Jews?

3. The term *Pharisees* has often been used by Christians as a catchword with many negative stereotypes attached to it. The term *Christian* has likewise been used in a similar way among Jews. Why do you think this might be?

Chapter 15: The Talmud

1. Why are there two different Talmuds, and how do they differ?

2. What can Christians today do that will aid their understanding of both the Jewish roots of their faith and the Talmud?

3. Scan the excerpt from the *Pirkei Avot* (Teachings of the Sages) on pp. 144-146. Does this help you understand the Jews' reverence for the Torah? What is meant by the phrase, "Build a fence to protect Torah"?

Chapter 16: Messianic Expectation

1. What changes do Jewish people think will happen for Israel and for the world when the Messiah comes?

2. How is the hope in the coming of the Messiah related to the belief in the resurrection of the dead?

3. How are Christian and Jewish hopes for a future time of salvation and restored harmony the same? What are the differences?

Chapter 17: The Old Testament: Jewish Book and Christian Book

1. Do you agree or disagree that the essential key for interpretation of the Old Testament is that Jesus fulfilled the Scriptures? What other approaches are there to interpreting the Old Testament besides the theme of fulfillment?

2. Do you think it is a good idea for Jewish scholars and Christian scholars to listen to one another's interpretations of the Bible? What do you think might be some of the outcomes of this?

3. Within Christianity there have occasionally been moves to reject the Old Testament as Christian Scripture. The church has always opposed these attempts. Why do you think the Old Testament should be considered as Scripture for Christians as well as Jews?

Chapter 18: Jesus the Jew

1. Why is it essential that Christians recognize that Jesus was a devout Jew?

2. What is it about Jesus that gives him his uniqueness for Christians?

3. What do you think are some reasons why the majority of Jews have never believed that Jesus was the Messiah? Do you agree with the statement on page 165, "The faith of Jesus unites us, faith in Jesus separates us?"

Chapter 19: Passover and the Lord's Supper

1. In recent years it has become popular in some Christian circles to celebrate a "Christianized" version of the Passover meal (*seder*). Do you think it is appropriate for Christians to do this? Why or why not?

2. In the Passover festival, the people are to think of themselves as personally having been freed from Egypt, as having been brought out of bondage into freedom. How does that enhance the meaning of the Passover for participants? What implications might it have for a Christian understanding of the Lord's Supper?

3. Both the Passover and the Lord's Supper have to do with "the memory of a deliverance, with redemption, and with a reenactment of saving events and fellowship at a meal which is the visible sign for the coming fellowship in the kingdom of God." Discuss what each of these mean, first for the Passover and then for the Lord's Supper.

Chapter 20: The Trial of Jesus

1. Do you agree that all human beings have a share in the guilt of Jesus' death? Why or why not?

2. If your church hymnbook includes the hymn, "My Song Is Love Unknown," read the text of that hymn together. Do you think this hymn singles out the Jews as having been guilty for Jesus' death? Does it show signs of self-righteousness?

3. In the fourth century, Matthew 27:25 was interpreted as a curse by the Jews on themselves for all time. How would you interpret this passage?

Chapter 21: Anti-Semitism

1. What attitudes did you grow up with concerning Jews? How has your study of this book affected your thinking?

2. How has the persecution of Jews through history been similar to or different from the persecution of other racial and ethnic groups? Are you aware of past or present examples of intoleration of those who are different in your community?

3. What are some things that Christians can do to work against anti-Semitism and other kinds of discrimination today?

Chapter 22: The Holocaust: Mass Murder of the Jews

1. After a tragedy of such unimaginable proportions as the Holocaust, is it still possible to think of human beings as gradually improving? Does either optimism or pessimism about the condition of human beings square with the view of the Bible? How do Christians understand human nature?

2. What can be done to ensure that an event like the Holocaust never again occurs?

3. What events in today's world give evidence that hatred of other racial or ethnic groups is still a factor that could lead to further acts of genocide?

Chapter 23: Jewish Hope and Christian Hope

1. The book states that the Jewish expectation of deliverance is "completely tied up with the destiny of the Jewish people as a whole, with the land which has been regained, with the rebuilding of Jerusalem and the temple, and with a kingdom of peace for all people." Why do you think Jewish hope is so closely bound to these earthly realities?

2. Does it surprise you that Jewish faith includes belief in the resurrection of the dead (cf. Acts 23:6-10)? Is there a difference between the doctrine of the resurrection and the idea of "the immortality of the soul"? How would you describe the two?

3. Read Romans 9–11. How would you summarize Paul's understanding of the Christian hope for the Jewish people?

Chapter 24: Christian Witness among Jews

1. How would you describe the differences between (1) genuine Christian witness, (2) proselytizing, and (3) the kind of "brainwashing" that often happens to members of cults? How can Christians make sure that they are relying on the Spirit of God and not on pressure tactics when they engage in witness?

2. Do you know any Jews who are also Christians? How do they understand the relationship between their Jewish identity and their Christian faith?

3. What do you believe is an appropriate form of Christian witness among Jews? Which of the options identified in the World Council of Churches statement (pp. 213-214) would you endorse?

Chapter 25: Christians and Jews Today

1. There is no question but that Judaism and Christianity are two closely related religions. What is your feeling about including Islam along with them, and about calls for meetings of these three religious communities together?

2. Are there ways in which the insights you have gained from this book can be applied to the public worship life of your congregation?

3. What opportunities are available in your area for becoming better acquainted with Jews? Consider taking the initiative in becoming personally acquainted with Jewish persons through a synagogue visit or a neighborhood discussion group.

Recommended Resources

The standard reference on Judaism is *The Encyclopaedia Judaica* (Jerusalem: Keter, 1972ff.), a multivolume work with periodic supplements.

For a clear and helpful book on all aspects of Judaism, see Leo Trepp, *Judaism: Development and Life*, 3rd. ed. (Belmont, Calif.: Wadsworth, 1981).

The following are recommended as readable and reliable resources:

Part 1: Introducing the Jews; Part 2: Israel—People, People of God, Country, and Land

John Bright. *A History of Israel*. 3rd. ed. Philadelphia: Westminster, 1981. (A clearly written treatment of the Old Testament period.)

Max Dimont, *The Jews in America*. New York: Simon and Schuster, 1980. (Easy reading, interesting presentation of the topic.)

Abba Eban. *My People*. New York: Random, 1984. (A history of Israel by one who played an important part in the modern period of that history.)

Abraham J. Heschel. *Israel: An Echo of Eternity*. 2nd. ed. New York: Farrar, Straus and Giroux, 1987. (A beautifully written appreciation of Israel.)

Chaim Potok. *The Chosen*. New York: Fawcett, 1986; *The Promise*. Fawcett, 1986; *My Name Is Asher Lev*. Fawcett, 1986. (Three fast-reading novels which give an excellent notion of what it is to be a Jew, described by an insider.)

Isaac B. Singer. *A Day of Pleasure: Stories of a Boy Growing Up in Warsaw*. New York: Farrar, Straus and Giroux, 1969. (A compelling account of Judaism in Poland by one of the great contemporary Jewish storytellers.)

Leon Uris. *Exodus*. New York: Bantam, 1981. (The birth of modern Israel in an exciting tale.)

Bernard L. Vigod. *The Jews in Canada*. Saint John, N.B.: available from Canadian Historical Association, Ottawa, 1984.

Elie Wiesel. *Night*. New York: Bantam, 1982. (Unforgettable account of a 14-year-old boy's experiences in the death camps of World War II.)

Elie Wiesel. *Souls on Fire*. New York: Summit, 1982. (The story of Hasidic Jews, with a generous supply of memorable Hasidic stories.)

Part 3: Jewish Worship; Part 4: Jewish Teachings

Judah Goldin, translator. *The Living Talmud*. New York: New American Library, 1957. (A portion of the Talmud, the "Teachings of the Sages" (*Pirkei Avot*), in a fresh and readable translation, with introduction.

Rabbi Jules Harlow, trans. and ed. *Siddur Sim Shalom: A Prayerbook for Shabbat, Festivals and Weekdays*. New York: The Rabbinical Assembly, 1985. (A new edition of the worship book for the Conservative community.)

Abraham J. Heschel. *The Sabbath*. New York: Farrar, Straus and Giroux, 1975. (Poetic and sensitive treatment of one of the central topics in Judaism.)

Michael Strassfeld and others. *The Jewish Catalog: A Do-It Yourself Kit*. Philadelphia: Jewish Publication Society, 1973. (A fresh and breezy presentation of Jewish life and teachings; second and third catalogs are also available.)

Herman Wouk. *This Is My God*. New York: Pocket Books, 1983. (A very readable presentation of Judaism by a playwright and novelist.)

Part 5: Jesus; Part 6: Christians and Jews

Edward H. Flannery. *The Anguish of the Jews: Twenty-Three Centuries of Antisemitism*. Rev. ed. New York: Paulist, 1985. (A classic study of the history of anti-Semitism.)

Leon Klenicki and Geoffrey Wigoder, eds. *A Dictionary of the Jewish-Christian Dialogue.* Studies in Judaism and Christianity. New York: Paulist, 1984. (A number of important topics, treated by both Christian and Jewish scholars.)

Pinchas Lapide and Ulrich Luz. *Jesus in Two Perspectives.* Minneapolis: Augsburg, 1985. (A dialogue between the Jewish scholar Lapide and Christian New Testament scholar Luz.)

Pinchas Lapide and Jürgen Moltmann. *Jewish Monotheism and Christian Trinitarian Doctrine.* Philadelphia: Fortress, 1981. (Another dialogue between Lapide and a leading Christian theologian.)

Elie Wiesel. *One Generation After.* New York: Schocken, 1982; *Legends of Our Time.* Schocken, 1982. (Two collections of shorter writings by the 1986 winner of the Nobel Peace Prize.)

Part 7: Statements on Jewish-Christian Relationships

Helga Croner. *Stepping Stones to Further Jewish-Christian Relations.* New York: Paulist, 1977; *More Stepping Stones to Jewish-Christian Relations.* Paulist, 1985. (Collections of statements from Roman Catholic and Protestant church bodies from around the world on Jewish-Christian relationships.)

Films and Videocassettes

For an up-to-date listing, call or write to one of the offices of the Anti-Defamation League listed on pp. 269-273. The items listed below are all available from the ADL. Especially recommended are:

"Avenue of the Just." (The story of Christians who saved Jewish lives during the Nazi period. 55 minutes, 16mm and videocassette, color.)

"The Camera of My Family: Four Generations in Germany: 1845–1945." (The story of the effects of the Holocaust on an upper middle-class German Jewish family. 18 minutes; filmstrip or videocassette.)

"Night and Fog." (A classic film on the Nazi death camps; in French, with English subtitles. 31 minutes, 16mm, color.)

"Scenes from the Holocaust." (Sketches made by Jewish artists in the death camps. 10 minutes, 16mm, color.)

For Further Information and Assistance

An excellent source for printed, audio, or video materials, as well as for information, is the Anti-Defamation League of B'nai B'rith. United States national and regional offices are listed below.

In Canada, contact: Cooperative Association with the League for Human Rights of Canadian B'nai B'rith, 15 Hove St., Suite 210, Downsview, Ontario M3H4Y8 (416) 633-6227.

U.S. National Office
823 United Nations Plaza
New York NY 10017
(212) 490-2525

Arizona Regional Office
The First Interstate Tower
3550 North Central Ave., Suite 1520
Phoenix AZ 85012
(602) 274-0991

Central Pacific Regional Office
121 Steuart St.
San Francisco CA 94105
(415) 546-0200

Connecticut Regional Office
1162 Chapel St.
New Haven CT 06511
(203) 787-4281

D.C./Maryland Regional Office
1640 Rhode Island Ave. NW
Washington, D.C. 20036
(202) 857-6660

Eastern Pennsylvania/Delaware Regional Office
225 South 15th St.
Philadelphia PA 19102
(215) 735-4267

Florida Regional Office
150 SE 2nd Ave. Suite 800
Miami FL 33131
(305) 373-6306

Florida West Coast Regional Office
5002 Lemon St., Suite 2300
Tampa FL 33609
(813) 875-0750

Greater Chicago/Wisconsin Regional Office
222 West Adams St.
Chicago IL 60606
(312) 782-5080

Jewish Community Relations Council
Anti-Defamation League of Minnesota and the Dakotas
15 S. 9th St.
Minneapolis MN 55402
(612) 338-7816

Long Island Regional Office
98 Cutter Mill Rd.
Great Neck NY 11021
(516) 829-3820

Michigan Regional Office
163 Madison Ave., Suite 120
Detroit MI 48226
(313) 962-9686

Missouri/Southern Illinois Regional Office
10922 Schuetz Rd.
St. Louis MO 63146
(314) 432-6868

Mountain States Regional Office
300 S. Dahlia St., Suite 202
Denver CO 80222
(303) 321-7177

New England Regional Office
72 Franklin St., Suite 504
Boston MA 02110
(617) 542-4977

New Jersey Regional Office
513 W. Mt. Pleasant Ave.
Livingston NJ 07039
(201) 994-4546

New York City Regional Office
823 U.N. Plaza
New York NY 10017
(212) 490-2525

New York State Regional Office
65 South Broadway
Tarrytown NY 10591
(914) 332-1166

North Carolina/Virginia Regional Office
1703 Parham Rd., Suite 204
Richmond VA 23229
(804) 288-0366

Northwest Texas/Oklahoma Regional Office
12800 Hillcrest Rd., Suite 219
Dallas TX 75230
(214) 960-0342

Ohio/Kentucky/Indiana Regional Office
1175 College Ave.
Columbus OH 43209
(614) 239-8414

Orange County Regional Office
2700 N. Main St., Suite 500
Santa Ana CA 92701
(714) 973-4733

Pacific Northwest Regional Office
1809 7th Ave., Suite 1609
Seattle WA 98101
(206) 624-5750

Pacific Southwest Regional Office
6505 Wilshire Blvd., Suite 814
Los Angeles CA 90048
(213) 655-8205

Palm Beach County Regional Office
324 Datura St., Suite 223
West Palm Beach FL 33401
(305) 832-7144

Plains States Regional Office
333 S. 132 St.
Omaha NE 68154
(402) 333-1303

San Diego Regional Office
7850 Mission Center Ct. #207
San Diego CA 92108
(619) 293-3770

South Central Regional Office
535 Gravier St., Suite 501
New Orleans LA 70130
(504) 522-9534

Southeast Regional Office
3384 Peachtree Rd. NE, Suite 660
Atlanta GA 30326
(404) 262-3470

Southwest Regional Office
4211 Southwest Freeway, Suite 101
Houston TX 77027
(713) 627-3490

Western Pennsylvania/West Virginia Regional Office
Allegheny Bldg., 7th Floor
429 Forbes St.
Pittsburgh PA 15219
(412) 471-1050

Index of Scripture Passages Cited

Index of Scripture Passages

Index of Names

Index of Subjects

Acknowledgments

Scripture quotations unless otherwise noted are from the Revised Standard Version of the Bible, copyright 1946, 1952, and 1971 by the Division of Christian Education of the National Council of Churches.

Excerpts from *Siddur Sim Shalom: A Prayerbook for Shabbat, Festivals, and Weekdays,* edited, with translations, by Rabbi Jules Harlow, copyright 1985 by The Rabbinical Assembly, are reprinted by permission of the publishers, The Rabbinical Assembly and the United Synagogue of America.

Excerpts from *Mahzor for Rosh Hashanah and Yom Kippur,* edited by Rabbi Jules Harlow, copyright 1972 by The Rabbinical Assembly, are reprinted by permission of the publisher, The Rabbinical Assembly.

Excerpts from *The Kuzari: An Argument for the Faith of Israel,* by Judah Halevi, copyright © 1964 Schocken Books Inc., are used by permission of Schocken Books Inc.

Excerpt from *O, the Chimneys* by Nelly Sachs, copyright © 1967 by Farrar, Straus & Giroux, Inc., is reprinted by permission of Farrar, Straus & Giroux, Inc.

Excerpt from *Night* by Elie Wiesel, translated by Stella Rodway, copyright © 1960 by MacGibbon & Kee is reprinted by permission of Hill and Wang, a division of Farrar, Straus & Giroux, Inc.

Specified selection pages 85-87 from *The Rise of David Levinsky by Abraham Cahan,* copyright 1917, 1945 by Abraham Cahan. Reprinted by permission of Harper and Row, Publishers Inc.

Photos: Religious News Service, 64, 94, 103, 119; Editorial Development Association, 67.